Basic cooking

All you need to cook well quickly

Jennifer Newens and Sebastian Dickhaut

Basic cooking
Contents

Think Basic
That's all you need to know

Basics: a plain white T-shirt and a little black dress. A pair of cool boots and diamond ear studs. Broken-in jeans and a beat-up leather jacket. Whatever. The fact is if you've got some of the basics, the rest takes care of itself. Whether you're just looking for something sort of hip or want to be really elegant, you can do it easily, as long as you have the basics.

Hold on—isn't this a cookbook? Absolutely. Lasagna and risotto, roast chicken and crab cakes, spicy guacamole and homemade mayo, and even chocolate pudding. All of them are basics. Things you can serve up anytime. Things that provide the substance behind your own individual style. Get the basics right and the rest takes care of itself—whether you're just looking for something sort of hip or want to be really elegant.

We wanted to put together a cookbook—another one, can you believe it! This time though, it's no "Joy of," no food encyclopedia, no great work of art. You won't find a thousand and one recipes here. No 2000 variations on a theme. Just all-time favorites, dishes worth the wait, and basic recipes, about a hundred and fifty in all, to inspire you to come up with your own.

So here it is: a cookbook for a kitchen full of ravenous friends, or for a desert island with a handy shipwrecked galley. A book to remind us that eating's vital for survival—which is exactly why it shouldn't always be taken so seriously. Just read on, whet your appetite, and get cookin'. And remember: Think Basic. That's all you need to know.

Know How

Joe: "It's fun to eat!"
  Jane: "No kidding."
Joe: "Going to the store's fun, too."
Jane: "You've got to be joking!"

Why should the people on TV have all the fun?
We see them lounging around the penthouse with a cup of

steaming coffee all morning, popping the lasagna into the oven at lunchtime, and laughing with their friends around the dinner table. You can do this, too. But there's a catch: You have to go shopping first—that's one thing they don't show you on the sitcoms. You never see the actors browsing along the supermarket shelves, pushing their way through the produce section, or checking out the price of a bottle of wine before it goes in the cart.

But in real life, that's what we end up doing at the store nearly every day. And, as you know, you can get pretty stressed out doing it. There's another way to do it without all the pain.

Sure, you don't get the true reward from the shopping experience until you eat. But why not anticipate the pleasure while you're still shopping? Just remember these three basic rules of smart shopping:

Believe in your abilities. Plan ahead. Be flexible!

Smart Shopping

75% of Americans don't know halfway through the day what they're going to have for dinner. How smart is that?

Just going to the store can do a body good. Toss what you crave into the cart and maybe a few treats, too—why not? But this is not a good long-term plan. The next day you always seem to have the all the wrong stuff in the fridge. And your money's gone so fast. Remember the 3 rules of smart shopping and you're halfway there.

Believe in your Abilities

Sounds like school. But this time it's about your own kitchen. If you feel confident that you can whip up something tasty from that leftover bell pepper, yesterday's rice, and a bottle of soy sauce, dinner will no longer seem like a chore. And if you know a good place where you can get fresh fish on the way home from work, you can create a quick paella for tonight's menu.

The true food lover always has a few standard bits and pieces on hand in the cupboard to rustle up a good meal. Read on—you'll find out more about these in the next few pages. These basics, together with our recipes and a half-hour at the store, are all you need to create a great, simple meal at home.

In order to make good choices with a minimum of hassle, you first have to know the difference between good food and bad food. Is money a problem? Are you a fussy eater? That's all OK. But then at least you have to know what's not good...Hard beans are not good. So if you're in a pinch, canned beans with a splash of balsamic vinegar will always be a better choice than trying to cook dried beans from scratch. And meat that comes out tough is definitely not good. Even if money's an issue, don't even think about gnawing on that cheap cut of meat—better just order in a pizza. Or buy a good piece of organic meat in the first place—it'll be cheaper in the long run—especially if you eat-up the leftovers...And asparagus in November isn't a good or a smart purchase. It's just common sense really: fruits and vegetables taste best when they're in season—and they're plentiful and cheap. They're especially good if they're not imported from far away. And as a bonus, you'll help boost the economy by supporting your local growers.

Plan Ahead
(but not too much)

75% of all Americans don't know at four in the afternoon what they're going to have for dinner. Then they often just grab a ready-made meal from the store on their way home. That's not very creative, and the expense can get a little out of control.

Let's plan a bit better than that. Some people make grocery lists for the whole week. All you have to do is think a bit about what you're going to eat today and jot a couple of things down. The shopping list is still the best way to go about it. You can use the back of an old receipt or an old page from your daily planner. The main thing is to hang on to it till you get to the checkout stand.

Smart shoppers divide up the work: one corner of the list for the meat and fish counters, one for the produce section, and another for the general supplies. They list their frozen food needs in one spot, dairy in another, and deli in another—this really maximizes their time at the store.

Be Flexible

OK—now it's time to just go out and do it. And if you come across something that would work better than what you planned, or is a better deal than what you had in mind: go for it. Believe in your abilities; you've planned ahead. And you can enjoy the luxury of just forgetting it all. No worries.

3 Golden Rules
of smart shopping

1 Eat something before you go

If you go to the store hungry, you'll buy too much. And that can get expensive. But it's also true that if you eat till you're stuffed, you might not want to think about food and just get outta there. That's not good either.

2 Take your time but don't waste your time

If you can avoid it, don't go to the store when you're in a hurry because you're more likely to grab anything off the shelf. That can get expensive, too. On the other hand, if you take a stroll down every aisle you can end up with more things in your cart than you intended. So focus is the key word here.

3 Keep your eyes open

Right-hand shelf, eye level—that pound of coffee will cost you more than fifteen bucks. But just bend your knees—and you'll find a pound for nine bucks. Now, eyes left—there you go, there's the flour. The first item you see is usually the most expensive. So look again. You'll find something cheaper. And you'll only find what you're really looking for after a long search. The moral is: watch out or you'll find your cart's full of very expensive stuff that you don't really want.

Think big

Singles know this already–unfortunately for them...the smaller the package the more expensive it is (per unit). Sometimes it really doesn't matter if you buy the small or the large pack of crackers. And it's often cheaper to buy food that's not packaged than tiny, prepackaged stuff—check the bulk food section for a better deal.

Cool basics

"Dear Joe,
It's time for a
little spring-
cleaning. The
food in here's
all in the
wrong place!
Love,
your fridge"

What do raisins and sauerkraut have in common? You don't have to keep them in the fridge. That's because back in the old days when there were no refrigerators, some smart dude figured out how to preserve them. Those days weren't so bad, you might think, savoring your scrumptious marinated olives. But refrigeration is a good thing. Otherwise the Chardonnay we're sipping now would be really warm and unpleasant...

Behind that door, the climate ranges from a mild winter chill in the fridge to an arctic blast in the freezer. But many foods prefer spring temperatures.

Microclimates in Your Fridge

In a regular fridge the temperature ranges from 32°-50°F. But it doesn't matter whether you've got a minibar with an ice tray or a luxury side-by-side unit with a champagne compartment, the back and the bottom spaces of your fridge will always be cooler than the front and top shelves. So, as a general rule of thumb, set your most perishable items, like fish, on the shelf right at the bottom and in the back towards the evaporator unit. Anything else? Three things: 1) It can also be really cold right next to the ice compartment if it is right at the top of the fridge. 2) It's warmer than you think in the crisper compartments where you keep the vegetables–the shelf on top stops the cold air from sinking further. 3) The climate is pretty mild in the fridge door and it gets warmer each time the door is opened.

The Freezer

Zero degrees Fahrenheit and colder–that's the temperature in the freezer—bitter cold, so you can barely move. Life in the deep freeze is caught in a time warp, which means food stored there will keep for longer. That doesn't mean it'll keep forever, though. Air and water still do their thing in here, even if it is in slow motion. The delayed aging process of hibernating food can be slowed down even more if the food is packaged so it's airtight. You can see what happens if it's not packaged properly if you check out a half-open bag of frozen French fries: you're soon left with a couple of dried out spuds and lots of ice crystals. Some people think that frozen vegetables are more nutritious

than those sold at the produce market. Might be true if the store is making money by selling old produce and shoveling it around like coal. Otherwise, it's always better to buy fresh. Peas or pasta from the freezer are really practical, though, and it's the perfect place to keep those 3 bowls of leftover soup. But: a fresh fish fillet or a tender steak are not really ideal for your deep-freeze stash— they belong in the pan right now!

Some Like Fresh Air

Many fruits and vegetables don't like fridge temperatures. Some, like bananas, just hate the cold (they'll turn instantly black); many, like tomatoes, permanently lose their flavor and texture; others, like melon, don't like it too cold for too long, but if they are briefly chilled before they are served they are really refreshing.

That Little Storage Label

What the storage instructions really mean:
• Keep cold: keep it in the fridge
• Keep cool: doesn't have to be kept in the fridge. It's better kept in a cool place at a maximum of 64°F.
• Keep at room temperature: store at 64-71°F(i.e., keep it in the cabinet)
• Protect against heat: can be stored at higher temperatures, but don't put it next to the oven or radiator
• Keep dry: keep in an airtight container, but not over the stove
• Keep in a dark place: store in cans or dark glass containers in the cabinet

Basic supplies in the fridge: what stays fresh and where

Top and Middle

A cheese for sandwiches and topping baked dishes (like cheddar) a cheese for grating (like Parmesan) a cheese for snacking (like Brie, blue cheese, soft spreading cheese), and fresh cheese, such as mozzarella, goat, etc., to use whenever.
How to store: keep in an airtight container, wrapped tightly in plastic wrap or in a locking plastic bag. Store strong cheese separately. Store fresh cheese or mozzarella in the original packaging.
How long: depends on the cheese, 3 days to 2 weeks, or until the sell-by date

Milk, cream, yogurt, buttermilk, sour cream, mascarpone, and crème fraîche
How: store in the middle of the refrigerator rather than the top; re-seal well after opening, always use a clean spoon to scoop out portions
How long: until sell-by date, 2-5 days once opened

Bottom
(the coldest spot)

Meat, fish, cold cuts
How: store meat and fish out of the original packaging on a plate or in a dish (not quite airtight); store poultry separately; keep cold cuts out of the original packaging in an airtight container, each item separate as much as possible; keep smoked items in a separate container
How long: raw ground meat no more than 1 day, raw poultry and chopped meats 1-2 days, other meat 2-3 days; cooked meat or poultry 3 days; fresh fish 1-2 days, smoked or marinated fish (once opened) 2-3 days, cooked fish 2-3 days; cold cuts 2-4 days, smoked meats 1 week or more

Door

Butter, eggs, opened jams, condiments, and beverages
How: in the right door compartments
How long: butter and eggs until sell-by date

Vegetable Crisper

Basic vegetable supplies of all kinds, like leeks, green onions, carrots, cabbage, and beets. Chinese cabbage, romaine lettuce or chicory keeps longer; stock up on ever-useful mushrooms and soup vegetables; otherwise items will depend on season, preference and your mood.
How: store loosely, keep delicate items not quite airtight in plastic wrap or a damp cloth; discard unusable green parts
How long: leaf vegetables and mushrooms 2-3 days, roots like carrots or beets 1-2 weeks, anything else 1 week

Herbs like basil, parsley, and chives are always good to have at hand; dill, tarragon, oregano, rosemary, sage, thyme, and chervil for special dishes
How: wrapped in plastic wrap or a damp cloth
How long: delicate items 2-3 days, everything else 4-7 days

Fresh Berries
How: separate from other foods, store berries loosely packed, preferably in a spot where they can be covered with a damp cloth
How long: 1-3 days

Freezer

Peas, spinach, chopped herbs; French fries, pastry dough, partially baked goods (brown at home), frozen fish fillets, frozen shrimp, frozen berries, ice cream, ice cubes; homemade dishes you can pep up and serve in an emergency
How: airtight in freezer containers and bags (re-seal opened items)
How long: until sell-by date, once thawed same as fresh items; baked goods 1-3 months, fish 3-6 months, fruit and vegetables 6 months (e.g., berries) to 12 months (e.g., carrots), meat (poultry, pork) 6 months to 12 months (lamb, beef); home-made dishes 3-6 months

Unrefrigerated

Eggplant, cucumber, potatoes, garlic, bell peppers, tomatoes, zucchini, onions; apples, bananas, kiwi, citrus and other exotic fruits
How: in a dark place (unless the fruit needs to ripen) that's airy and dry. Potatoes, garlic, onions 45-60°F, vegetables 45-60°F, fruit 55-65°F. Fruit and vegetables can make each other spoil faster (e.g., apples when stored with potatoes, pears, bananas; citrus with avocados, apples, and bananas)—so store these items separately.
How long: depending on temperature, just a few days (fruit), 1 week (vegetables) or 2 weeks (potatoes etc.)

Basics
in the Pantry

Joe: "I have nothing to eat!" Jane: "But the refrigerator's full!" Sound familiar?

Imagine the following: A luxury cruise with amazing food. Suddenly you hear a big bang. One hour later, you wake up on a deserted tropical island. And you're starving. Fortunately, the ship's galley floated to shore, and the large palm tree over there has an electric outlet. Too bad all the food is at the bottom of the ocean! No more eating to your heart's content. "Wrong," whispers a silky voice. A mermaid! "I can provide you with three ingredients. Choose carefully. Think basic." "Okay," you say. "How about some pasta? Or maybe bread?" "Pick flour," whispers the ocean muse. "Yeah, of course! And some salt!" you reply. "No, no, no," the mermaid shakes her head pointing to the salty sea. "How about some garlic?" she suggests. "Good idea," you answer. "And some butter. I've gotta have some butter!" "In this heat?" she scolds. "Some olive oil?" you offer. "You finally got it, she says. Now farewell and good luck!" "Wait a minute," you shout. Don't you want to eat something first? How about I whip up some spaghetti *aglio olio*?" "OK," concedes the mermaid. But I'll take care of the wine."

From M to XL- Basic Supplies for Everyone

Think basic. That's easier said than done when it comes to basic food supplies. Why not stockpile a bunch of food? That's a concept from an earlier century, as nowadays you can buy complete candlelight dinners at almost every convenience store. It might be nice once in a great while, but prepared dishes from convenience stores or supermarkets can get old real fast.

What about a compromise? Stock up on some of the basics, and then shop for the rest of your supplies as you need them. You can adapt this technique to your individual appetite. But first, ask yourself some questions: How often do I sit down at the table and who with? Is it only the little mermaid, or do I want to allow for other vacation acquaintances once in a while? And what about personal tastes?

To start, we recommend purchasing some basic supplies in size M as in "Musts." These are all the basic staples that you need to survive in an average North American household. Then, we can look at supplies in size L as in "Luxuries." Here you'll find everything you need to give flavor to your life. "Extra-Lavish" supplies come in size XL: these are everything else that you love, even if you are the only one.

Quality in Storage

Some say that the kitchen is the worst storage area for foodstuffs. While it is true that kitchens—with their changes in temperature and many different odors—are not always the ideal storage place for groceries, pretty much everyone stores their food there. It's simply the most practical way to do it. How about the basement? Too far. The root cellar? What's that? The cool bedroom at the back of the house? Who wants to sleep with dried peas?

Anything that does not need to go in the refrigerator can last for a little while in the kitchen. Some precautions are advisable, however: keep the stuff away from heat (store it away from the stove), dry (in well-sealed containers), and most of all away from light (in sealed tins, dark glass containers, behind closed cupboard doors).

About Shelf Life

Anytime you find "best until..." Or "consume by..." on a food package, the manufacturer guarantees that the product will be almost unchanged by that date. However, most products are perfectly fine for a slightly longer time period. Bouillon cubes, for example, may just take a little longer to dissolve after their use-by date. In general, it is safe to assume that a short shelf life means it takes a short time after the consumption date for the product to begin to deteriorate seriously.

All you need for the Basic Kitchen, how to store it, and how long it will keep

Best until...: Translation–As long as it tastes good
Almost forever: Translation–Still OK after 12 months

M as in "Musts"

Sugar, Salt
Keeps almost forever in sealed containers

Flour, Rice, Cornstarch
Keeps for over a year in dark, sealed containers. Whole-grain flours keep for a somewhat shorter time period

Cornmeal and Bread Crumbs
Store like flour, but for 8 months only

Oatmeal, Cereals
In dark and airtight containers for 6 months

Pasta
Store in a dark area. Dried, it will last for 1-2 years

Sandwich Bread
Packaged until consumption date, open for about a week

Milk
Until expiration date, opened, refrigerated for 3-5 days

Coffee
Store in a dark, airtight container until expiration date

Curry Powder, Nutmeg, Paprika, Pepper, Cinnamon
Store in a dark, sealed container. Ground spices will stay fresh for up to 1 year

Dried Herbs
Store in a dark and dry place for 6 months

Instant Broths and Sauces
Powdered keeps almost forever; cubed for 6-8 months

Oil
In the dark for 1 year; opened bottle, somewhat less than 1 year

Vinegar
Store in the dark; keeps almost forever

Tomato Puree, Ketchup, Mustard
Until expiration date; opened refrigerated for several weeks

Soy Sauce
Store in a dark area; keeps for almost a year

Pesto
Until expiration date; open for a month, refrigerated and covered by a layer of oil

Olives
Until expiration date, opened for several weeks

Pickles
Until expiration date, opened refrigerated for 1-2 weeks

Tuna and Canned Beans
Until expiration date, opened refrigerated for 1-3 days

Canned Fruit, Jam
Until expiration date, opened refrigerated for 1-2 weeks

Honey
Lasts almost forever in a dark area. Crystallizes with time.

Raisins
Dark and dry place for 1 year

Chocolate and Cocoa
Until expiration date and longer

Almonds, other nuts
Dark and dry place for 6 months

Vanilla Extract
Keeps aroma for 1 year in a closed bottle

Baking Powder
Until expiration date and longer

Wine
Dark and cool place. Good for at least 1 year after bottling. Some wines almost forever. Opened, 1 day to 1 week

Fresh Bread (unsliced)
Keeps in a dark, dry area with air circulation for 2-10 days, depending on type of bread

Potatoes, Onions
In a dark, airy, dry place for 2-3 weeks

Garlic
Store like potatoes

L as in "Luxurious"

Risotto Rice
Keeps for 1 year in dark and sealed container.

Cookies and Crackers
Until expiration date, opened for 1-2 weeks

Espresso
Store in a dark and airtight container until expiration date

Capers
Until expiration date; opened, refrigerated for several weeks

Dried Chiles, Cumin, Cloves, Juniper Berries, Cayenne Pepper, Ground Ginger, Dried Marjoram
Store in a dark and dry place for 1 year

Specialty Oils, such as Olive
Store in a dark place away from heat for 6-12 months, depending on variety

Specialty Vinegars, such as Balsamic
Store in a dark place for 6-12 months, depending on variety

Tabasco, Worcestershire, and Hot Sauces
Store in a dark place, almost forever

Prepared Horseradish, Canned Anchovies, Anchovy Paste
Until expiration date; opened, refrigerated for several weeks

Pepperoncini, Sun-Dried Tomatoes in Oil
Until expiration date, open, refrigerated for about 2 weeks

Applesauce
Until expiration date; opened, refrigerated for 1-2 weeks

Yeast
Until expiration date

XL, as in "Extra Lavish"

Cornmeal
In a dark, sealed container for 6-8 months

Curry Paste
Until expiration date; opened, refrigerated almost forever

Mango Chutney
Until expiration date; opened, refrigerated for several weeks

Coconut Milk
Until expiration date; opened, refrigerated for 1 week

Pumpkin Seeds and Pine Nuts
Store in a dark container, refrigerated, for 6 months

Dried Mushrooms
Store in a dark and dry place almost forever

bacon

shrimp

cheese

stock

lemon

garlic

tomatoes

soy sauce

pesto

balsamic vinegar

curry

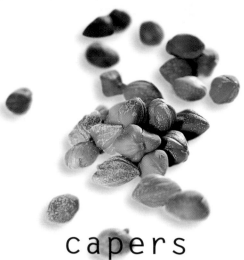

capers

bread

the
17
staples
for the
Basic
kitchen

parsley

honey

chocolate

mustard

Bacon

French: lard; Italian: lardo; Spanish: tocino
Comes from the belly, leg or back of pigs; is cured or smoked. Good bacon is mostly meat, without much fat, tasting of meat and smoke before salt. Not bad on bread, if you like that.
Ideas : fried bacon on salads • pasta flavored with bacon and cream • sautéed bacon with wine for an interesting sauce • wrap meat with bacon before sautéing • wrap a chicken breast with bacon before grilling • top a casserole with strips of bacon • wrap chicken livers, figs, or cheese with bacon—bake for fast tapas

Shrimp

French: crevettes, Italian: gamberetti, Spanish: camarónes
Shrimp are worldly animals with many names. We mean the common cocktail variety, cooked and peeled. They're difficult to find fresh, but frozen is a good alternative to have on hand for instant meals. Avoid canned shrimp. They should have a nice ocean flavor and be without the dark veins. Best prepared when steamed or sautéed gently for a short period of time.
Ideas : potato salad or fried potatoes with shrimp • salad with garlic oil, sautéed shrimp, and croutons • bruschetta with shrimp, tomatoes, and pesto • scrambled eggs with shrimp • steak with fried shrimp

Cheese

French: fromage; Italian: formaggio; Spanish: queso
Originates from milk from cows, goats, sheep, or buffalo. Comes in many forms, from fresh cottage cheese, to moldy blue, to creamy white, or hard for grating. Flavor can be mild as butter or strong as stinky feet. Cheese can be good for anything as long as it is natural (i.e., not processed).
Ideas : salad dressing with cottage cheese • vegetable gratin with ricotta cheese • oven-grilled bread with Camembert • cheese sauce with pasta • grated Parmesan with spinach and carrots • grated Swiss cheese in vegetable soup • fried or scrambled eggs with crumbled feta • fresh mozzarella with caramelized fruit

Stock

French: fond, bouillon; Italian: brodo; Spanish: caldo
Whether made from beef, chicken, fish, or vegetables—stock should be a basic in every household. Homemade stock is ideal, frozen in small portions for ease—try an ice cube tray for kicks. See basic stock recipes on pages 66, 78, 82, 99.
Ideas : touch up vinaigrette with stock • steam potatoes in stock • boil noodles in stock • use stock instead of butter in mashed potatoes • for fast sauces use stock instead of water • stock with grilled bread and grilled onions for a super-fast onion soup • chicken stock with lemon

Lemon

French: citron, Italian: limone, Spanish: limón
Very basic: Available all over the world and in your corner store. Good for cooking, baking, blending, garnishing. Its juice is fresh and tangy and brings out flavor. Lemon zest adds old-time goodness to desserts and rejuvenates limpid sauces.
Ideas : enliven salads with lemon juice • refine soups and sauces with lemon juice • add lemon zest to goulash • flavor fish with peeled lemon slices • add lemon zest to fresh berries to top vanilla ice cream • make lemon sugar: add thin pieces of lemon zest to the sugar bowl; more intense: rub sugar cubes with lemon zest

Garlic

French: ail, Italian: aglio, Spanish: ajo
Garlic is sensual and health giving–but disliked by some people. Certainly not by Basic Cooks. Gives its heady aroma to all healthy kitchen pleasures. But: old, dry or sprouted garlic can have a nasty taste. Even nastier: garlic powder. Cool: garlic breath (provided that both of you have it).
Ideas : mince garlic to give punch to anything • rub the salad bowl with garlic before tossing • use a garlic clove on a fork to scramble eggs • simmer potatoes or rice with garlic and bay leaves • use whole roasted garlic cloves as a toasted bread spread

Canned Tomatoes

No translation
Sometimes even star chefs will grab a can, particularly a can of peeled tomatoes, which often have more cooking power than fresh. Whole, they work well for slow cooking; in chunks, for fast-cooked things; tomato puree gives concentrated aroma.
Ideas : make a spread for crackers from butter, tomato puree, Parmesan, garlic, and basil • braise stuff in peeled tomatoes and their juice—very Italian • top toast with salami, cubed tomatoes, and mozzarella • steam fish with peeled tomatoes • simmer canned beans with cubed tomatoes to go with grilled chicken

Soy Sauce

French: sauce soja; Italian: salsa soia; Spanish: salsa soja
Just as most villages in Europe brew their own beer, so every Asian village has its own soy sauce, made from fermented soybeans. Asian cooking freaks often have many types in their cupboards: dark, strong and salty soy sauce from China, aromatic-sweet soy sauce from Indonesia, and light mild soy sauce from Japan.
Ideas : dipping sauce made from soy sauce, rice vinegar, ginger, and garlic • enhance chicken stock with soy sauce • spike grilled fish with soy sauce • marinate meat in soy sauce before grilling • flavor grilled mushrooms with soy sauce

Pesto

No translation
Once upon a time only Ligurian mammas spiced up their food with this paste made from basil, garlic, pine nuts, olive oil, and Parmesan cheese; today pesto has a cult following the world over. The closer the ingredient list is to the original, the better and more expensive the pesto. Our Basic recipe is on page 89.
Ideas : potato or pasta salad with pesto • pesto, tomato, and mozzarella sandwich • gnocchi with pesto • bean-tomato soup with pesto • grilled eggplant with pesto • grilled chicken rubbed with pesto • cold roast beef or chicken with pesto • fresh cheese mixed with pesto as a dip

Balsamic Vinegar

No translation

Good balsamic vinegar is made from long-fermented grape juice, and is aged in wooden barrels. The best is at least 12 years old, labeled "tradizionale." The price: It's more expensive than other vinegar. If not, it will also have the same taste as other vinegar. Look for "Modena" on the label for the real stuff.

Ideas: bruschetta with Parmesan and splashes of balsamic vinegar • finely cut mushrooms with balsamic vinaigrette • steak juices enhanced with balsamic vinegar • white wine sauce finished with balsamic vinegar • potatoes braised in balsamic vinegar • strawberries with basil and balsamic vinegar

Curry

No translation

Comes in powder or paste form. If it's good curry, meaning it's hot and pungent, it will enliven your food with its Asian mystique. Though different with every cook or manufacturer, the basics of this, the most famous spice blend in the world, are: turmeric (makes it yellow), cloves, cardamom, coriander, cumin, nutmeg, fenugreek, cinnamon, and chiles—which determine the curry's level of heat. Needs to be cooked in fat for best flavor.

Ideas: sauté onions with curry for rice pilaf • fish soup with curry and coconut milk • tomato soup with curry • curry with lamb • curried yogurt • use as a marinade for grilling • steam vegetables with curry

Capers

French: câpres; Italian: capperi; Spanish: alcaparras

You either love or hate them. Old proverb: He who loves the blossoms of the caper bush knows happiness. Pickled in brine, they keep their particular flavor almost indefinitely. The smaller the caper the finer the taste. Tiny "nonpareils" are almost like caviar. Caper berries with the stems attached are good on the tapas platter.

Ideas: vinaigrette with capers • caper butter with garlic, parsley, and lemon zest • cottage cheese with pesto and capers • tomato sauce with capers and tuna • cold cuts in a sauce made from capers, cream, and mustard • salmon tartare with capers

Bread

French: pan; Italian: pane; Spanish: pan

Thinly sliced bread can be a lifesaver. Slice by slice, it is always ready in the freezer, to spring to life immediately with the help of a toaster. Use for canapés, croutons, toast points, bread crumbs...

Ideas: brown bread cubes in butter or olive oil until crisp and use as croutons on salad • spaghetti with garlic and toasted bread crumbs • quick casserole: mix toasted bread cubes, ham strips, and eggs and bake in the oven • quick French toast: dip bread in 1 cup milk beaten with 2 eggs, vanilla, and cinnamon, and fry until golden brown

the 17 staples for the Basic kitchen

Parsley

French: persil; Italian: prezzemolo; Spanish: perejil

Frizzy parsley is still used as decoration on cold-cut plates to give you something to laugh at. It's the flat-leaf or Italian parsley that's the secret ingredient for many chefs. For example, my friend Pete makes a divine parsley pesto when the basil's not looking so good. Parsley's pretty leaves make it our green supermodel.

Ideas: flat-leaf parsley salad with cherry tomatoes • hot apple chutney with parsley • parsley pesto (page 89) with pasta • parsley cream soup • Asian soups with floating fresh parsley sprigs • gnocchi with parsley • half spinach, half parsley as a side dish

Honey

French: miel; Italian: miele; Spanish: miel

Honey is a natural sweetener, with different aromas based on its origin—from resinous flavors originating in wild forests to the more neutral kind from clover meadows. Cold-processed honey retains more natural flavors than heat-processed honey, but it's more expensive and is a complete waste of money if you plan to cook with it.

Ideas: raw vegetables with ginger-honey cream cheese • red cabbage salad with honey vinaigrette • baked goat cheese with honey • chicken wings marinated in honey and soy sauce • honey-mustard with dill over shrimp • whipped cream with wild honey on raspberries

Chocolate

French: chocolat; Italian: cioccolata; Spanish: chocolate

Dark chocolate belongs in every Basic kitchen. Even if you prefer milk chocolate for eating, semisweet or bittersweet chocolate is ideal for cooking and baking, as it is purer—with at least 50% or more cocoa solids than milk chocolate. Another good basic: pure cocoa powder (look for "Dutch-processed")

Ideas: heat chocolate with cream, chill, and whip until stiff for chocolate whipped cream • make chocolate curls using a vegetable peeler • mix chocolate chunks into cake batter and/or cookie dough • dip fresh strawberries into melted chocolate • add cocoa to pancake batter

Mustard

French: moutarde, Italian: mostarda, Spanish: mostaza

As with soy sauce and honey, there are many different types of mustard. Pick a good, basic mild variety for your everyday needs, and add a stronger and/or hotter type when you want to spice things up. Sweet mustard is a popular choice for dips and spreads, and grainy mustard works well on cold foods.

Ideas: apple salad with creamy mustard dressing • cold sliced meat spread made from hot mustard, minced pickles, and crème fraiche • smoked salmon rolls with mustard • sausages with grainy mustard on a baguette • fresh fish basted with mustard before grilling

Basic
cooking techniques

"I am going to make myself some food."
The question is, how?

Let's take potatoes. You can boil them, with the peels or without, in water or in stock. But you can also fry them in slices, in cubes, or whole. And bake them. And braise them. And grill them, steam them, smoke them, and deep-fry them. HELP! This sounds like too much work.

Remember: Think basic. You can't do everything at once anyhow, and the goal when cooking is always the same: To get something raw hot enough so that it's easier to eat and tastes better. Water and heat—in the form of electricity or gas—are the key tools. Depending on how you use it, water can cause pliability, or result in diluted, faded flavors. The right amount of heat will determine the texture of the food. Too much heat will result in a charred disaster.

Think of cooking as a continuum—a lot of water and a little bit of energy is called poaching, which gives you soft, tender textures. No water and a lot of energy is called searing, which you use for crispy crusts. Between these extremes lies the world of cooking. Welcome.

Strong Cooking

Also known as boiling or blanching, what we refer to as "strong cooking" is cooking using a large amount of both water and heat. Items cooked with this method need a lot of moisture and high cooking temperatures over a short period of time. Think of cooking pasta and broccoli.

Basic Supplies for Strong Cooking

We use strong cooking for a range of different foods, from the family-sized package of spaghetti at dinner to the soft-boiled egg at breakfast. For these and everything in between, basically two pots are necessary: one for the small items, holding about a quart of water, and one for larger items with a capacity of 4-5 quarts. If you cook frequently, you might want to have two additional pots—a small one with high sides that holds about a half-gallon of soup, and a large flat one holding 3 quarts, for boiling potatoes.

Expensive special equipment is not necessary for strong cooking. On the other hand, since you'll probably use your Basic Pot for more than just boiling water, it shouldn't be just any old tin camping pot. Stainless steel is always a good choice. Enameled pots can also last for a long time. Look for a pot with a heavy bottom, as it will heat more evenly and prevent burned spots while cooking. It is also important that the pot fits your burner—especially if you have an electric stove—for optimal heat distribution. The handles of the pots should take even low oven temperatures (i.e., not plastic) in case you want to use them for braising. Also make sure the pot has a tightly fitting lid so that the heat will stay inside the pot.

What else do you need for strong cooking? A wooden or metal spoon for stirring, a ladle to dish things out, and a colander for draining things. And salt—lots of salt.

Salt is Essential

Strong cooking usually takes place in salty water, which brings out the flavors of the food. You could use a different liquid, but why? A good-quality stock wouldn't flavor pasta much during its short boiling period. Particularly for blanching (we'll explain that in a minute) you need a good quantity of salt in the pot to make sure that the food will get its proper share during the short cooking time. A tip: bring the water to a boil, throw in the raw food, and then add the salt—this will bring things back up to a boil again fast.

Pure Cooking

A chef or cookbook may offer strange recipes for deep-frying pasta or smoking duck in a wok. But what we are talking about here is the purest form of cooking—boiling in 212°F bubbling water. The objective: completely cooked food—perhaps with a slight bite at the center—and without a crust. What to do in a nutshell: get things very wet, quite hot, and for only as long as needed. What happens: with pasta, the starch swells until it's just done; for vegetables, the cell structure loosens. However, if the boiling goes on for too long, firmness turns to mushiness and flavor dissipates into nothingness.

Strong cooking has one disadvantage. Nutrients and aromas can be lost during its contact with the water. For this reason, some people believe that steaming is a better solution than boiling. However, since steaming takes longer than boiling there could be an even greater loss of flavor with delicate foods. It's better to cook with enough hot water so that the bubbles don't stop

1

when the food is thrown into the pot, and get the whole thing over with as quickly as possible. It is also important that the food pieces are of the same size and consistency.

Cooking Pasta

Use 1 quart of water for every 4 ounces of pasta. Fill a pot with water (at most 3/4 full) and bring the water to a boil over high heat. When the water's boiling rapidly, add the pasta and about a teaspoon of salt. Stir vigorously—stickiness can be a problem in the beginning. Make sure the water comes to a boil again and stir from time to time. No lid required (1).

The cooking time depends on the type of pasta, but the time should be indicated on the package. Dried pasta normally takes 8 to 13 minutes. Toward the end of the directed cooking time, capture one of the noodles and take a bite. Try it several times if you need to (2). If it's too hard, keep on cooking. You're aiming for something called *al dente*. Translation: the pasta should be soft most of the way through, but have a slight resistance on your teeth at the middle. Once it's ready, throw everything into a colander to drain away the water.

Purists now mix the pasta with the sauce and put the hot bowl right on the table—you don't need to shower the pasta with cold water. If you have to, you can run hot water briefly over the pasta. But the main rule is: The guests and sauce can wait. Pasta, never. Also, remember to avoid cold plates when serving pasta. Tip: Just before the pasta is done, ladle some of the spaghetti water over the plates to warm them up.

Cooking Potatoes

Scrub the potatoes thoroughly with a vegetable brush under running water. Put them in a pot of cold, salty water. Bring the water to a boil and continue boiling for about 20 to 30 minutes. Stick a knife in a potato or eat a piece to tell if they're done. When cooked, drain the potatoes through a colander, put them back in the pot, and set the pot back on the burner—to drive out some

of the remaining steam— for about 1 minute. If desired, remove the skins while potatoes are still hot. Secret of success: make sure the potatoes are approximately the same size so that they will all be done at the same time.

If you prefer to peel your potatoes before cooking, that's OK, too. Peel clean raw potatoes and remove any dark spots with a paring knife. Cut the peeled potatoes into pieces of similar size. Put the pieces quickly into a pot of cold salt water (if they don't hit water fast they'll turn brown). Follow the cooking instructions above, but reduce the cooking time to 15 to 20 minutes.

Cooking Vegetables

Put equal-sized pieces of beans, broccoli, asparagus, or other vegetables (make sure they're all the same type) into a pot filled with plenty of boiling salty water. Cook them until done—the time will depend on the type. The best way to tell if they're done is to eat one. Drain the water through a colander. For delicate vegetables, use a skimmer to fish out pieces and let the water drip away.

Blanching (partially cooking vegetables) is even faster than boiling. Cook the vegetable pieces in rapidly boiling salted water only for a short time, just to begin the cooking process. Quickly drain them, then plunge them into ice water (3). This cold shock keeps the vegetables' color brilliant and helps retain their consistency, but takes some of the flavor away. It's a must, however, when making vegetable casseroles, gratins, or quiches.

Gentle Cooking

Gentle cooking, AKA poaching and simmering, unites extremes—both the roughest and most tender pieces of meat, poultry, and fish benefit from cooking just under the boiling point. From filet mignon to beef shank, boneless chicken breasts to stewing hens, whole fish to fish dumplings—gentle cooking is the most versatile of cooking methods.

Gentle Cooking Supplies

Actually, you really don't need different pots for strong and gentle cooking. Just make sure they're the right size. For gentle cooking, this means that the food pieces shouldn't touch the edge of the pot, or be lost in the cooking liquid. For poaching chicken breasts (we'll tell you about it soon), a small pot with a long handle is perfectly sufficient. For cooking larger pieces of meat, like a pot roast, or a bunch of dumplings for your friends, a larger pot is needed (holding 5 quarts or more).

Things that take gentle cooking need to be handled carefully. This is especially true for fish, which cooks best just covered by liquid in a flat pot—which makes it easy to get at when the fish is done. If you frequently cook larger chunks of fish, a flat, oval fish poacher might be a good investment—it's also great for cooking asparagus.

During gentle cooking, don't use a fork for testing doneness or for removing the food from the pot—you'll hear this again when we talk about searing. Instead, use a ladle, skimmer, or lifter with holes (1) so that everything stays in one piece. Often during gentle cooking, you'll use the cooking liquid as part of the meal. For this reason, a ladle and sieve are important.

It's All in the Liquid

As in strong cooking, gentle cooking uses water as its main cooking medium—especially when cooking large items, like a whole chicken, for long periods of time. Other ingredients, such as spices, herbs, and vegetables, are added later during the cooking process for flavor. For a shorter gentle cooking process, it is better to prepare a full-flavored cooking liquid ahead of time, so that the flavors can infuse into the food during the brief cooking time. For example, fish fillets are poached in a stock made from water, wine, onions, vegetables, bay leaves, a few peppercorns, and lemons.

Simmering and Poaching

When simmering, the temperature of the cooking liquid should ideally be about 185°F—not below 176°F. Anything lower than that could spoil the food. Anything above 200°F tends to come awfully close to the boiling point. Poaching is a bit subtler than simmering, using slightly lower temperatures.

How do you know if you are simmering or poaching properly? There's no need to get out a thermometer. When simmering, you should occasionally see tiny bubbles at the surface of the cooking liquid. Keep things going in this manner and your food will stay tender and juicy. If you're poaching, look for a slight quiver on the surface of the liquid. Bubbles here are a no-no, but there should be some steam rising off the surface of the liquid.

Remember: big bubbles are your worst enemy during gentle cooking. Simply put, If you use strong cooking for things that need gentle cooking, it will result in an unappealing breakdown of the food's cell structure. For

The outside of the meat will be flexible to the touch, with a tender, juicy interior. Add salt on your plate.

If you want to serve vegetables, add them about one hour or more before the meat's done. You can also add bay leaves, and a couple whole cloves and peppercorns.

You can use the same technique with a stewing chicken. Make sure the water is not boiling when the chicken goes into it—otherwise the skin will tear and the chicken will dry out. The chicken will take about 1 to 1½ hours.

Poaching Fish

Fish should be protected by as much skin as possible to keep the juices inside. The more skin, the better the fish will taste after poaching. That's why whole fish are particularly well suited for poaching, as well as thick steaks cut from such fish as salmon or tuna. However, with a well-flavored cooking liquid, even skinless fish fillets can taste great poached.

Bring a good fish stock (see page 82) to a boil and pull the pot off the burner. As soon as everything in your pot is peaceful, place the fish inside the pot—not too many pieces and never one on top of the other. The stock shouldn't be allowed to cool down too much (2). Now put the pot back on the burner and poach the fish. Something should be happening to the stock, but only under the surface, which should remain calm. The fish will be done in 6-9 minutes, depending on type and thickness. Tender chicken or pieces of filet mignon can also be poached in this manner.

Follow the same instructions for whole fish, making sure your poaching pot is the right size. Large whole fish, such as salmon, need to be started in cold stock, to make sure that the heat gets distributed evenly. Smaller fish, like trout, should be started in hot stock. For small whole fish, poaching can take 5-8 minutes; for bigger ones, it could take as long as 10-20 minutes.

example, meat boiled too vigorously will become stringy and tasteless. With fish, you need to be even more careful. Fish immediately falls apart in boiling water and becomes bone dry. Therefore, when cooking fish, it is important to get the cooking liquid up to the correct temperature rapidly and keep it there. First aid for your pot: Have a cup of cold water next to your stove, just in case the liquid starts boiling.

Simmering Beef

You'll need about 4½ pounds of lean beef. After the long, slow cooking time, you'll be left with a great stock. If you prepare a stock ahead of time by boiling a few bones for an hour, your stew will turn out even better. The best cuts of beef for stewing are from the chuck, shank, or rib areas.

Now it's actually quite simple: Add onion and a little garlic to a pot of water, (about 1 quart of water per 1 pound of beef—no salt) and bring gently to a boil. Then, add the meat and keep the temperature very low—so the liquid does not bubble but starts to show a slight movement just under the surface after about 20 minutes. Keep that movement going without any sudden wild bubbles for about 2-3 hours, and everything will turn out just fine.

Vapor Cooking

We're talking about two different things here, but both involve cooking in the vapors generated from the cooking liquid in a covered pot. You're already familiar with steaming. But there's another useful concept in the Basic kitchen. Instead of boring you with the fancy French term, let's just call it "low-low cooking"-read on to find out why we named it that.

Vapor Cooking Supplies

For low-low cooking, the lid is more important than the pot. The lid should seal well enough to keep the vapors and liquids inside the pot, so that the different flavors can be fully developed in this warm and humid environment. Any simple pot will do, large enough so that the food can pretty much rest in a single layer on the bottom—that way everything will get done at the same time.

You can use the same type of pot for steaming, as long as it's tall enough to accommodate a coffee mug and saucer (more details on this later). If you steam often, consider investing in a specialized 3-part pot made exclusively for the purpose of steaming foods. Steamer inserts for regular pots, such as a stainless steel or Asian bamboo basket, are even better. In a pinch, a stainless steel colander (without a handle) can be used, provided that the lid can still fit tightly on the pot.

A Little Liquid

Low-low cooking is a question of give and take: The liquid you use gives heat and sometimes flavor to the food to be cooked, and the food gives nutrients and always flavor to the cooking liquid. As a result, both end up on the plate. The more concentrated the liquid, the stronger it tastes. The liquid can be spring water (real snobs use only their personal brands), stock, wine, cream, or a pre-made sauce. For steaming, normal tap water is fine, but herbs and spices will add flavor here as well.

In Haze and Steam

Are you dying to know what we mean by low-low cooking? Truth be told, it's hard to define. Is it braising? Stewing? Or perhaps a cross between poaching and steaming? Remember: Think Basic. The bottom line is that food is being prepared with a little bit of liquid and a little bit of heat. In other words, it's a low-liquid, low-heat cooking method—low-low cooking. A few vitamins and aromas might be lost in the cooking process, but they'll get absorbed into the cooking liquid, which is incorporated into the finished dish.

When we talk about steaming, the picture is much clearer. Water is boiled, and the steam generated by it surrounds the food and cooks it. The advantage: Pure flavor. Almost nothing gets lost, as is the case with boiling. However, some people believe that steam, too, can destroy nutrients and

vitamins, since it's hotter than boiling water, and that steaming takes longer than boiling. Nevertheless: What you lose to heat and cooking time is probably less than what is leached out during boiling.

Low-Low Cooking Vegetables

Almost every vegetable can be cooked in this manner, with the exception of legumes. It is important that all the pieces are first cut the same size. If everything works perfectly, the cooking liquid will become a concentrated essence, combined with *al dente* vegetables.

Based on how much cooking time is required, you'll need different quantities of liquid. For example, carrots are just covered in liquid (1), while spinach leaves only need the drops of the water used for washing them when they're placed in the pot. As we said before, a closed lid is essential for low-low cooking. If the pot is very full, occasional stirring is needed so that every piece gets exposed to the vapors and cooking liquid.

Here's something special: Glazed vegetables. The same cooking principles are used, but butter provides the cooking liquid, rather than water. A dash of sugar is also needed. For the last few minutes of cooking, the lid is removed, and the vegetables are cooked just a bit longer until they're covered with a shiny syrup (glaze). If you like, you can stir in a bit of fresh butter at the end for flavor. Slightly sweet vegetables, like carrots, taste heavenly cooked this way. Also great: Use cream, which tastes delicious with leeks.

Low-Low Cooking Fish

Blend 1 cup of fish stock (page 82) and a half-cup of white wine in a pot, add a few onion slices, and boil for about 2 minutes. The bottom of the pot should be covered by a finger's width of liquid. Remove the onions. Add salted fish fillets or small whole fish to the pot so that they sit in a single layer in the pot.

Turn the heat to low and cover the pot with a lid (you can also place a piece of buttered aluminum foil directly on top of the fish). The fillets will be done in 2-6 minutes, while whole fish might take as long as 10 minutes. Remove the fish from the pan, then stir in a little crème fraîche to the cooking liquid, and you have a wonderful sauce. For a complete dish, prepare vegetables ahead of time in the same way and keep warm.

Steaming Vegetables

Bring some water to a boil in a pot or the bottom of a steamer. Place a steamer insert or the perforated steamer layer over the boiling water. Place the vegetables on the insert or perforated layer and seal the whole thing with a lid. It's important that the water is not too close to the food to be steamed, or that you don't try to cook large piles of vegetables at a time. The cooking time depends on the type of vegetable, but it will take about 30% to 50% longer than when boiling. Seasonings are added once the food is done.

Steaming Fish

This works best in an Asian bamboo steaming basket—look in a specialty or Asian foods store for one. Line the basket with lettuce or cabbage, add herbs and spices, and put the fish on top—ideally whole fish, to which you've cut a few slits in the skin on both sides (2). You can also do this with fish fillets.

Now, boil water in a large pot to generate steam and set the covered basket in the pot. A 1-pound fish will be done in 15-20 minutes, fillets in 5-6 minutes.

Anything else? Oh yes, the trick with a coffee cup for occasional steamers (3): Put the cup upside down in a pot with a little boiling water, set a plate with the fish on top of the cup, close the lid, and steam. Very Basic!

Skillet Cooking

Here we're talking about sautéing and searing. Sautéing (sometimes called pan-frying) is a cooking method in which food is cooked quickly in a small amount of fat over direct heat. Pretty basic. Searing, a variation of sautéing, is a way of cooking meat and fish over high heat so that it gets a tasty crust, and seals in the food's natural juices. As you may have guessed, skillet cooking requires a skillet (AKA frying pan).

Two Skillets, One Spatula

The Basic kitchen needs two skillets. One for light, sensitive stuff, and another for tougher things. Lighter foods, such as fish, vegetables, and eggs, are best prepared in a nonstick skillet. There are many brands and models on the market, but they all serve the same purpose: What goes in should come out, without anything sticking to the surface. Stirring with metal implements or cleaning with scouring pads will scratch the coating on the skillet, harming its nonstick qualities. Even more important is not to let the skillet get too hot. Above 500°F in the oven may destroy the nonstick coating—in spite of the 3-year guarantee. Anything else? Perhaps look for a skillet with a heavy bottom—this will hold in the heat better and won't get bent out of shape.

For searing, you need pure metal. Nonstick skillets should not be used. Professionals use cast-iron skillets—maybe you've gotten hold of Grandma's. Household skillets are mostly made of stainless steel. Other alloys are also available. Here, be extra sure your skillet has a heavy bottom. After repeated use, these skillets will smooth out and develop a natural nonstick quality. Once a metal skillet has been "seasoned," or broken in, it can become invaluable. Avoid abrasive sponges and harsh detergents when cleaning them, as these tend to damage the surface.

A spatula is essential for skillet cooking. Imagine a steak, beautifully seared on one side. You go to flip it, and stick the prongs of a fork into the crust. The delectable juices, previously sealed in, start to seep out into the pan. Wouldn't a spatula have been a better choice?

Fats for Skillet Cooking

For pan-frying things like eggs and delicate fish fillets, butter works well. Olive oil and clarified butter can take more heat. When things get really hot, vegetable oils are best. A sliver of butter or some extra virgin olive oil can always be used towards the end of cooking to add additional flavor.

Skillet Cooking 101

Sautéing—you see it all the time in cookbooks. But how, exactly, do you do it? Here's it is in a nutshell: Put a skillet on a burner over medium to medium-high heat. Add the fat and get it hot. Add the food (you should hear a sizzle). Cook, stirring frequently, until the food is done. It's that simple.

Searing is like sautéing, only a little more intense. It's usually meat or sturdy fish that gets seared. But what happens during the searing process? When the meat or fish is put into the hot pan, the protein fibers on the surface congeal

1

immediately and a protective skin forms, which eventually turns into a delicious crust. The interior is cooked with a slower, more even heat.

Two things can interfere with searing: Smoke and water. Smoke results from a skillet that is too hot—easy to take care of. On the other hand, if you try to sear at a temperature that's too low, the protective skin does not form fast enough to keep the food's juices inside. Boiling will result, and the fish or meat will end up dry.

To avoid either terrible situation, heat the skillet first without any fat. When it's hot, add the fat, which will heat up rapidly without burning. A hissing sound when adding the meat indicates the right temperature. It's best to first test with a corner of the meat or fish you're searing. Also, watch the amount of fat. If there isn't enough fat in the skillet, the food can burn rapidly. Too much fat results in too low a cooking temperature, too much liquid, and dry food.

Sautéing Fish

Before cooking, fish fillets should be rinsed in cold water, patted dry, and seasoned with salt. Dredging the fish in flour (remember to shake off the excess) will create a light crust, which gives a little stability to the fish fillet.

Now, add fat to the skillet, set it over medium heat, and put the fillet into the skillet with the prettiest side down. Cook the fish until it's brown on the underside, and then turn it over. Cook it until the other side is browned and the fish is cooked through. Fish is done faster than you think. When it's opaque all the way through and flakes easily when prodded with a fork, it needs to be removed from the skillet. Thick pieces, of course, take a little longer and therefore should be cooked at a slightly lower temperature to ensure that they cook through before the outside burns.

Searing Steaks

For a tender seared steak, a certain thickness is required—1½-2 inches is about right. You can season the meat with salt and pepper before or after searing— your choice.

Heat the fat in a skillet over medium-high to high heat, but make sure it doesn't start to smoke. When putting the steak in the skillet a good hiss should be audible (test a corner first). Let the meat cook, undisturbed, for a little over a minute—check to see that it has a nice brown crust. Turn the meat over and sear for another minute. Remove the pan from the heat and let it stand for a few minutes.
Then, continue sautéing the meat over medium heat (1-3) for a few more minutes, turning the steak several times, until it's cooked to the desired doneness. Thicker steaks can take higher heat.
Let the meat rest for a few minutes after cooking, wrapped in aluminum foil (4) in order to redistribute all of its juices and keep it warm.

Oven Cooking

Now we're talking about roasting and braising. We're also mostly talking about meat, and usually meat that's not very tender. This kind of meat only really gets good after some time in the oven. If you've got the time to slow roast or braise your meat, you may as well go all out—invite a bunch of people for dinner, stick the roast in the oven, and then go back to bed for some beauty sleep before the party!

Heavy Metal

This time you'll need a bit more than your basic baking pan. But it doesn't have to be the world's most expensive top-of-the-line roaster, either.

What you need for this kind of production is a longish, heavy, flat-bottomed roasting pan with a lid—make sure it's roomy enough for your biggest roast. You want a really heavy pan so that things won't easily stick to the bottom and burn. Have a ladle and fine sieve ready for straining the scrumptious pan juices for the sauce.

Start with the Good Stuff

Lots of people think the best thing about a pot roast is the gravy—it'll be a real winner if you put only top-quality ingredients into the pot. Onions are almost always included, providing color and essential flavor. All sorts of diced root vegetables are also typical additions. Tomatoes add Mediterranean flair. Wine and stock add depth. Adding whole spices early on or herbs towards the end can give a special twist—the more subtle the flavor you want, the later you add them.

Slow is Good

When you're cooking in the oven, the same principle applies as when you're cooking on the stovetop: the more heat you use, the faster things cook. With lesser quality or tough cuts, the meat fibers are coarse and need some time to relax. After browning, the meat should be roasted long and slow in order to come out tender and juicy.

This is what happens when you roast a roast: first, browning releases hot juices from the food, which dry on the outside to form a crust. Now that the meat's surface is sealed, the remaining hot juices migrate toward the center of the meat, transferring heat and cooking the meat as they go.

However, when you braise a roast, the cooking liquid penetrates the whole roast, and the meat's juices seep into the cooking liquid. You're left with a tender, succulent piece of meat and lots of excellent gravy to serve at the table. If you're braising lots of small pieces of meat instead of one large hunk, the end product will be a like goulash or a stew. But the cooking principle's the same.

Roasting

Roasting refers to cooking in an oven in an uncovered pan, using dry heat as the cooking medium. The food is seasoned and then browned in hot fat (1)—either on the top of the stove or in a 475°F oven. Small, tender cuts don't need more than a quick searing; larger, tougher cuts can take longer—up to half an hour in fact.

There are two main types of roasting—let's call them "quick roasting" and "slow roasting." The oven should be set at 350°F and up if you're going the quick route; slow roasting can be done at 200-300°F, depending on what it is you're trying to cook.

There are two main things to remember when you're roasting: baste frequently with the pan juices so the crust doesn't burn; and after roasting, let the meat rest for a while so the juices deep inside the roast can redistribute themselves evenly and the meat fibers can relax a little.

Braising

Braising is a variation of slow roasting, but it incorporates a cooking liquid, and is done in a covered pan. Braising is the best way to go with lean, tough cuts of meat. Braising is a good thing to remember when you're on a budget—the tougher cuts of meat are usually cheaper.

First the meat is seared as described above in a pot that's not too large. Then vegetables are browned. It's all put together with liquid and spices. It's important not to cover the meat completely—only about halfway (see 2)—otherwise it'll boil instead of braise. Now, cover the pot and cook the whole roast in its own juices and steam, letting it simmer till done. Experts like to do this in the oven to get the most even cooking. But it works on the stovetop, too, if the meat is turned often.

Once the meat is done you can let it rest in aluminum foil in the oven (which is off) while you're making the gravy. Skim off the fat (see 3) and pour the ingredients through a fine sieve using the ladle to press everything through, then season it to taste.

Stewing

This is similar to braising a pot roast, only the meat is cut into pieces. First brown the meat cubes. If you have lots of pieces, do them in batches. Then sauté the vegetables—onions usually—until translucent, put the meat back in and season the mixture.

Now you have a choice: if you're going with a slow braise, like a beef stew, initially it only takes its own juices and a couple of splashes of water now and again for it to turn out beautifully tender. You add liquid only just before it's done. Things like chicken pieces don't take as long and are cooked in a large amount of liquid.

29

Wok Cooking

Now things are heating up. These methods of cooking, use very high heat, and either a little or a lot of oil. We're talking stir-frying and deep-frying. The temperature in the wok or deep fryer rarely dips below 300°F, so you need an able hand and a bit of skill. But there is a reward: with meat, fish, and vegetables you get a great crust on the outside; on the inside, your food will be very tender and delicious.

Hot Iron

What kind of wok should I pick? Depends: for stir-frying you really want a thin-walled one. Asian woks are made of sheet iron and usually have a rounded base, which conducts the heat well. This type will work even on a

gas stovetop—you can get a special ring for the wok to perch on. You can also buy a flat-bottomed wok that's perfect for an electric stove. Ideally a wok's diameter should be about 14 inches. Iron woks are inexpensive and do a good job, but the metal can buckle with repeated use. A thin stainless steel wok is a good alternative, but it can be very expensive. Or you can just replace your old iron one when it's time! When you're ready to wok and roll, you'll need a special wok spatula with a rounded edge to toss things in the pan, and a curved wok ladle to lift things out. You can find them where you find good woks. You don't need a lid to stir-fry, but you will for braising, steaming and boiling—you can do all these things with a wok, too.

What about deep-frying in a wok—Asian-style French fries?? Why not—you don't always need a deep fryer to fry in a oil-bath. Actually, using a wok means you can use less fat. For frying, you can also make do with a large pot, deep enough to half-fill with fat, leaving a large space to prevent splashing. You'll need a wire basket or sieve that fits in the pot to lift larger things out, and a skimmer to fish out more delicate things.

Wokking Essentials

A real stir-fry chef needs three fundamental things: garlic, ginger, and green onions. These are the usual suspects that appear in many stir-fried Asian dishes. And often spicy sauces and pastes—like soy sauce, fish sauce, oyster sauce, curry paste, or black bean paste—are added at the end to add a bit of punch. Forget any of these when you deep-fry because they burn instantly and will ruin the oil. The oil itself has to be able to stand a lot of abuse, so go for one with a high smoke point that's neutral in flavor. A basic vegetable, peanut, or canola oil is a good choice.

Heat is the Key

When you stir-fry, the hottest point is in the center at the bottom of the wok. This is where vegetables and meat gain an instant crust, sealing in the juices underneath. Small pieces cook really fast—each second counts. All the ingredients must be chopped or mixed ahead of time, ready to toss into the pot when it's time. It's also important to keep the food on the move; otherwise it'll quickly start to burn. You have to work like a whirlwind. Those in the know use the side of the wok (the higher you go the cooler it gets) to keep cooked things warm.

Deep-frying just means cooking by submerging foods in hot fat. Two things have to be just right for it to work: first, cut pieces small. Frying big pieces of food can cause the outside to burn while the center is still cold.

To prevent this, you can either pre-cook large items, or just cut them up smaller. Second, make sure you are using the right level of heat. If the oil is too cold, the crust won't form quickly enough and the food will soak up the fat. However, if the fat's too hot—as in smoking—everything will crisp up too soon, and the outside will be black when the center is cooked. Can you test the oil's heat without using a thermometer? Sure—drop a bread cube in it. If it's crispy golden brown in 1 minute, the temperature's right (1).

Wokking Vegetables

When wokking—AKA stir-frying—everything needs to be cut up ahead of time. Don't forget that the firmer the ingredient, the finer you need to chop it. For example, spinach gets coarsely shredded, but carrots should be very finely sliced. All this has to be done in advance, along with getting out the seasonings and the sauce. When you're wokking, that's all you've got time for.

Basic wokking: get it really hot. When a drop of water does a tap dance in the wok, it's hot enough. If it just sizzles and putzes around, turn up the heat. Now coat the sides of the wok with oil and put a tiny puddle in the bottom to heat. Throw the vegetables in, first the ones that take longest to cook. Cook the veggies, tossing the whole time with the spatula, so that nothing sticks. Now—in with the next batch of vegetables—the stuff that doesn't take quite as long—stir, toss, next batch, and so on and so on. If everything is evenly tender to the bite, then your timing was perfect. If not, it'll still taste great, and next time even better. Now you can add spices and sauces, stir well, and dish the stuff out onto plates.

Advanced wokking: Start as above, then stir-fry vegetable #1. When done, push it up the side of the wok. Throw in vegetable #2, stir-fry until done, mix with vegetable #1, and push everything up the side of the wok. Now for vegetable #3, and repeat the process. One thing's important with either version: don't add so much that the pieces end up on top of each other. You can stir-fry about a pound of vegetables like this.

Vegetable Tempura

Vegetables with a high starch content, like potatoes, deep-fry well. More delicate things, or ingredients with a high water content, benefit from being plunged into batter before frying.

Japanese tempura batter is great for vegetables. But before you make the batter, chop the vegetables into bite-sized pieces, then briefly parboil the really hard ones. Heat about 1 quart of oil to 350°F (see instructions on left). While the oil is heating, make the batter: carefully combine 1⅔ cups ice-cold water (preferably left in the freezer and taken out just before it freezes) first with 2 egg yolks, then with 1 cup of flour. Don't fret over any little lumps: stirring for too long or too vigorously will ruin the batter.

Now, dredge the vegetables first in flour, then in the batter you just mixed (2). Let the excess drip off, and lower pieces into the hot oil. If the surface is just coated, that's good, because otherwise the oil cools off too quickly. After 1-2 minutes, everything should be cooked and crispy, and now you can scoop it out with the skimmer (3), set it on paper towels to absorb the excess oil, and season with salt. (You can keep the vegetables warm in a very low oven, if desired). Bring the oil back up to the correct temperature and continue deep-frying the remaining vegetables.

knife

peppermill

cutting board

the
14
essentials
for the
Basic
kitchen

grater

whisk

kettle

electric

peeler

measuring tools

blender

can opener

corkscrew

strainer

citrus juicer

stereo

Knife

If you think that buying a big, cheap set of knives will make you a kitchen god/dess, better think again. As with many things, you get what you pay for. It's better to have a few high-quality knives that will last for a long time. You'll want a paring knife for the small stuff, and a bigger, all-purpose utility knife with a long, narrow blade for everyday cutting. One more knife is essential, one with a really big, wide blade that you can chop with without constantly hitting your hand on the cutting board. This comes in handy for slicing onions and chopping fresh herbs. True, this knife alone will set you back more than your bargain-basement set. But it will last you longer than the whole collection.

Peppermill

Freshly ground pepper or stale, preground pepper from a jar? People who don't care, probably think Moby Dick is sexy reading. Just-milled peppercorns taste much more than just spicy, adding many delicious nuances to your food. Every Basic kitchen needs a decent peppermill. But decent doesn't necessarily mean designer. Just take the thing for a test-drive to make sure it does a good job milling the peppercorns. Go for the funky old oak one that has an adjustable milling wheel and is easy to refill. Or would you rather buy that fancy Plexiglas pyramid that constantly slips through your wet fingers in the kitchen, and that is about as convenient to refill as breaking into a pharaoh's tomb? Remember: Think Basic.

Cutting Board

Maybe chopping tomatoes on the kitchen table is seriously rustic, but in the long run it just messes up your furniture. That's why the Basic kitchen needs a cutting board. In fact, you'd best get a second one for special jobs like chopping garlic so the fruit salad doesn't reek. Be sure to get one that's large enough to handle your cooking jobs. Plastic or wood are equally good—your choice. Things to avoid: grooves that are supposed to collect the cooking juices (things get stuck there), weird shapes (everything falls off) little feet for stability (a damp cloth below works better).

the
14
essentials
for the
Basic
kitchen

Grater

One word: Parmesan. Because freshly grated Parmesan makes pretty much everything taste good, Parmesan alone is why a grater is an absolute must in the Basic kitchen. The simplest model is best, i.e., the perforated shovel-shaped one with a handle. It's good to have at the dinner table next to a hunk of cheese, but it's also perfect for enhancing the cake with lemon zest. In a pinch, you can even scoop with one or use it for stir-frying. If this type of grater doesn't fit your needs, there's always the square box grater, which can also grate carrots, slice cucumber, and shred cabbage. Or, put a tea light inside and you have a great outdoor lamp!

Whisk

For all of your whipping and stirring needs, you only need one. Look for two things: springy wire and a comfortable handle. A good whisk will get lightness and air into the mix, and ensure that beating something doesn't turn into a session at the gym. It will also be easy to clean. And now a tip for hand-frothed cappuccino: heat some whole milk (skim milk is for wimps) in a small, high-sided saucepan, hold a whisk between the palms of your hands and twirl, twirl, twirl...The resulting foam will even hold sugar.

Electric Kettle

This might be a stretch, but once you have one of these hot pot-tea kettle hybrids, you'll wonder how you survived without one. Sleepyheads love them for boiling water so fast, they're sipping their early morning tea before their roomate beats them to the shower. Crazy cooks use it to bring a potful of noodles instantly to boil. Both types like the fact that it switches itself off and that you don't need the plug to be near the stove. Two serious warnings: Be careful of the steam. And always fill it adequately or it'll start to act weird.

Peeler

Even if Mom scraped the carrots and peeled the potatoes with a paring knife, a peeler with a loose blade is a huge improvement in the basic kitchen. Because it's so easy to peel cucumbers with it. And asparagus. Whether you hold the blade diagonally or vertically is more a question of your own style and motor skills. You need a bit of imagination when you use the peeler: Cut carrots lengthways like fettuccine. Or remove strips of cucumber peel diagonally for pretty slices. Lots of ideas....

Measuring tools

If you think measuring ingredients is too rigid, you either have too much red tape in your life, or are far too relaxed. Making custard without measuring properly can very quickly turn into a stressful experience. You don't have to go that route: a 2-cup liquid measuring cup, preferably transparent, can help. The more gradations the better. Anything smaller gets measured with a teaspoon or tablespoon. A shot glass (measuring 1-1½ oz) is also helpful. Dry measuring cups are also a Basic kitchen staple, ranging from 1/4 to 1 cup. Some good equivalents to remember: 3 teaspoons = 1 tablespoon; 4 tablespoons = 1/4 cup; 4 cups = 1 quart; 4 quarts = 1 gallon.

Blender

Forget fancy food processors. If you're lucky enough to own a hand blender, you might wonder how you lived without it. Press the button, and boom—your shake's mixed, your soup's pureed, and your sauce is emulsified. Of course, you need one that's not wimpy. Another good kitchen tool is your bar blender—yea, the one you use to blend up batches of margaritas. And don't forget: lots of things taste just fine without being blended to oblivion. Some things shouldn't be blended at all: blending makes mashed potatoes tough and slimy, makes herbs bitter, and cream too stiff before it has a chance to get some air into it.

Can Opener

Even though we in the Basic kitchen use lots of fresh produce, not much works without peeled tomatoes in the cabinet. For that reason alone you need a can opener. It doesn't have to be an electric model—unless you've got a Great Dane in the household. But it is important that it doesn't take excessive musclepower or brainpower to use. If the wheel is sharp, not the nut, that's the way to go—whether it's the super-fancy type or the old-fashioned version. And remember: can openers can—and should—be washed, too.

Corkscrew

This fancy big brother of the can opener is the more demanding of the two. But the same applies here as before—the less brainpower and musclepower required the better. Choose your personal favorite. The simple spiral model with the perpendicular handle is very basic, but it's really only any good if you have superhero strength. The waiter's corkscrew is a good, slim choice, but it takes a little practice to use properly. Another version (pictured) has an implement that holds the bottle while the "screw" penetrates the cork.

Strainer

The important thing about a strainer is its holes. A coarse strainer—commonly referred to as a colander—has fairly big holes to strain things quickly, or drain pasta or potatoes. A fine mesh strainer—sometimes called a sieve—is used for separating solid from liquid parts when making soups and sauces. (True kitchen snobs will then strain their stock through a paper coffee filter.) A sieve should be metal, but a colander need not be; many kitchens go for years with a $1.99 plastic colander for draining pasta and washing salad greens. But for salad fanatics, a salad spinner is a must. It combines a colander with a manual fan for clean, crisp salad greens.

Citrus Juicer

Every household already has at least two— each hand. But squeezing citrus juice maually doesn't get the very last drops out. Both standard and designer juicers have one thing in common: the cone that looks like the tip of a comic book rocket. It's this that presses the juice out of the fruit. If there is nothing to separate the seeds and pulp from the juice, that's not good. It's better if the juice can drip down through a filter into a small dish. Because using a juicer requires brute force, it's especially important that you choose one that's stable.

Stereo

A kitchen without a stereo is like a summer without sun: pretty dull. You can always find something suitable for your mood, or the occasion—opera for an Italian meal, salsa for a south-of-the-border fiesta, rock-and-roll for a BBQ. And if you have some boring prep jobs, you'll be glad to have some sing-along music blasting to distract you from your tasks. But be careful with gripping radio programs. If all the pots are rolling and steaks are burning because you're too engrossed in what you are listening to—better turn on some classical.

the recipes

basic

Noodl
Potatoes

Filling...easy to make...and loved by everyone...

es,
& more

Hungry? OK—we're almost there. We've spent a quarter of this book shooting the breeze, but now it's time to put something good on the table. So, no more dawdling—we want something to eat! Something satisfying, easy to make, and, preferably, that dirties just one pan. Of course, it also must be something that everyone likes.

Now, what would a hungry person do in Italy? Make pasta of course. But Italians like to make rice dishes too, for example, risotto. In Asia people eat lots of rice when they're hungry. But they like to cook piles of noodles, too, depending on the region. But Germany has to be the leader in bread consumption—nowhere else in the world can one find as many kinds of bread as in Germany. Bruschetta and crostini are popular right now—wait, aren't those Italian? We Americans love sandwiches, but also French fries when we're hungry—though French fries really come from France, or Belgium, actually. Potatoes are always a favorite for hungry people, in any form, from Idaho to Ireland! Holy cow—we're just plain hungry.

Let's get down to it and just eat!

All right, already.

Turn the page!

A World of Sandwiches

A hot dog in a bun can save you when you're hungry--well, that's really only true in U.S. ballparks, on New York City street corners, and in some parts of central Europe. The rest of the world turns up its nose at the thought of chowing down on a simple bit of bread and sausage. Real Italian calzone, an authentic French crôque, or a true-blue American sandwich must be jam-packed with goodies to be worthy of the name. Apart from that, anything goes. How about a skyscraper sandwich constructed from an international buffet of sandwich ingredients? That way everyone can grab a couple of slices to satisfy their own craving.

Melina's Sandwich
Pita bread spread with a paste made from chopped green olives and olive oil, topped with grated Romano cheese, grilled eggplant slices, marinated bell peppers, and crumbled feta cheese

Nadja's Sandwich
Whole-grain bread layered with lettuce and scrambled eggs, topped with cooked shrimp, garnished with thin strips of fresh ginger and shallots, and drizzled with soy sauce

Charles's Sandwich
A French roll stuffed with chopped apples, cornichons, and anchovies, slathered with mustard-mayo spread, and topped with sliced cooked ham

Gretel's Sandwich
Sliced sourdough spread with cream cheese, lettuce, and sliced tomatoes and eggs, topped with capers, chopped fresh chives, and a generous helping of freshly grated Parmesan cheese

Tom's Sandwich
White bread with strips of iceberg lettuce and chunks of roast chicken, in a creamy sauce made from plain yogurt, curry powder, mango chutney, and a smidgen of Worcestershire sauce—sprouts top it off nicely

Lorenza's Sandwich
A ciabatta sandwich layered with arugula, spread with a puree made from white beans and pesto, and topped with sliced salami and a couple of sun-dried tomato pieces

Pedro's Sandwich
A length of baguette lined with green bell pepper strips, chile peppers, and radicchio, spread with garlicky mayonnaise, and topped with chunks of tuna and grated cheese

Hot Rice

When cooking rice, remember: 1 cup of uncooked rice makes 3 cups of cooked rice. That's more than twice the rice, enough for a pair, or second helpings.

Rice swells as it cooks because the grains suck up all the cooking liquid. Once all the liquid has been absorbed, the rice is cooked just right—fluffy and flavorful. And it isn't hard to prepare at all.

Look for "converted" (parboiled) long-grain rice. Here's the basic method:
In a saucepan, bring 1 cup rice and 2 cups cold water or stock to a boil and simmer until all the liquid has just been absorbed—it takes about 20 minutes. Then, pull off the lid to let steam escape, fluff the grains with a fork, and that's it!

Even cooler is Middle Eastern-style rice pilaf:
In a saucepan, heat 1 tablespoon oil, pour in 1 cup of rice, and stir until the rice grains are opaque. Then, add 2 cups of liquid (water or stock), season with salt and pepper, place the lid on the pan securely, and simmer over medium heat for 10-15 minutes. Warning: Don't be tempted to look in the pot (steam will escape) or to stir the rice (it will unfluff) during the cooking process. Right at the last minute, take a quick peek into the pan. If the liquid has almost disappeared, and if the top layer of rice has little cavities in it– steam chimneys–remove the pan from the heat and let the rice stand, covered, for 10 minutes. Now you can stir the grains and serve your ultra-fluffy, tasty rice.

By the way, on page 51 you'll find another method for making rice pilaf, infused with lemon flavor.

Our Favorite Tummy Filler

Noodles

French: nouilles; Italian:
pasta; Spanish: fideo

Types of noodles:
• In Italy: spaghetti (long, thin), maccheroni
(small, tubular), rigatoni (short, hollow),
penne (hollow, cut diagonal), tagliatelle
(long, thin strips), fettuccine (long, wide
strips), linguine (long, narrow, flat), farfalle
(bowties), ravioli (stuffed pockets), tortellini
(stuffed and twisted pockets), and hundreds
more
• In Asia: cellophane noodles (thin,
translucent), rice noodles (long, fine), somen
(thin, made from wheat), ramen (thin,
instant), and udon (spaghetti-like)
• In the US: egg noodles, shells, and all of
the above

Noodles are:
• strength giving
• addictive—the more you eat, the more
noodle-dependent you become
• easy to prepare

Noodles need:
• constant cooking
• to be eaten right away
• lots and lots of sauce
• hot plates for serving

Noodles love:
• everything, really—from pats of butter to
slices of truffle
• sauces made from tomatoes, cream,
cheese, mushrooms, meat, or shellfish—
almost anything
• seasonings like garlic, fresh basil, fresh
cilantro, black pepper, shallots, fresh ginger,
soy sauce, and chile peppers

Baking or Boiling Spuds?

Apparently, there are some people who can whip up 37 different raviolis with one hand tied
behind their back, and order basmati rice from Karachi over the Internet. Pretty wild! Yet the
same people then go to the deli and grab a bag of any old potatoes to make mashed potatoes
like Mom used to make—and end up with a gluey mess in the bottom of the pot. Not very smart.

The right potato at the right time makes a huge difference in the success of a recipe. Some
varieties of potatoes don't have a very high starch content, so they stay firm and moist when
cooked in water. Let's call these boiling potatoes. They're great for boiled for salads, and
roasted as side dishes. Look for red potatoes, or round white potatoes.

On the other hand, boiling potatoes don't bind well—they have too much moisture and lack the
starch content you need to make great mashed potatoes or dumplings. Another type of
potatoes, baking potatoes, is very starchy, and cooks up with the proper mealy texture when
you plan to mash or whip them. Good baking potatoes include russets or Idahos.
A third type of potato is kind of a cross between a boiling potato and a baking potato. It won't
crumble when cooked, but still has plenty of binding starch. This type makes great cottage fries
or a base for a casserole. Yukon gold, yellow Finn, or long white potatoes are good choices.
Always be sure to check the label at the produce stand or on the bag for the name of the variety
and the type of potatoes you're buying.

In
knowing your Asian noodles and how to cook them • making spaghetti that doesn't stick •
serving polenta as an alternative to mashed potatoes • steaming basmati rice • pancakes
anytime • serving a multicultural selection of sandwiches • *Never out of style: boiled new
potatoes, mushroom risotto, crispy pizza*

Out
leaving noodles in the soup too long • cutting spaghetti • serving pasta with more water than
sauce • gnocchi with bland sauce • making risotto with sweet rice • toast...that isn't quite
toasted • calling pancakes "crêpes" • *Never, ever in style: the saying "it doesn't taste very
good, but at least it fills you up"*

Spaghetti alla Bolognese
The mother of all noodle dishes

Feeds 4:

1 onion

1 carrot

2 stalks celery

3½ ounces slab bacon

2 tablespoons butter

10 ounces ground meat (a combination of meat or poultry, if desired)

1/2 cup dry red wine (or meat stock)

1 small can peeled tomatoes (14.5 ounces)

1/4-1 teaspoon red chile flakes

Salt, freshly ground pepper

1 pound spaghetti

1 chunk Parmesan cheese (enough for this meal and then some)

1 Begin preparing everything that goes into the pan first: peel the onion and carrot, wash the celery stalks, remove the rind from bacon, and cut everything into small cubes.

2 Place a large skillet over medium heat and wait until the bottom of the pan is hot. Throw the cubed bacon into the pan and fry until there is almost no visible fat left. Add the butter and all of the cubed vegetables and sauté until the onion is translucent.

3 Push the vegetables and bacon to one side of the pan, making a space in the middle. That's where the ground meat goes; use a spatula to divide it into smaller portions and sauté for 2-3 minutes, until you're left with crumbles of meat.

4 Pour the wine (or stock) into the pan. Add the canned tomatoes (with the juice), crush them, and mix everything well. Add the chile flakes, together with one teaspoon each of salt and pepper. Simmer over low heat for at least 15 minutes, or up to an hour—why not? Stir frequently.

5 Time for the pasta: in a large pot, bring 5 quarts of water to a boil, and add 2 tablespoons salt. Once the water is at a rolling boil, shake the spaghetti from the box into the pot, using a cooking spoon to ease all of the pasta into the water.

6 Cook for 7-8 minutes with the lid off, then fish one noodle out of the water and taste it–spaghetti should never be too soft, nor too hard, but just slightly firm to the bite (*al dente*). If the sauce has thickened too much, add a couple of spoonfuls of hot spaghetti water to the pan at the last minute. When the spaghetti is done, pour it into a colander, give it a shake, and let it drain.

7 Taste the sauce, adding more salt and pepper to taste. Serve the spaghetti in deep dishes and pour the sauce generously over the top. Put the Parmesan chunk and a cheese grater on the table—that way everyone gets to grate their own fresh cheese over the steaming hot pasta!

Prep time: 45 minutes
Good with: French bread, green salad, red wine—preferably Chianti
Calories per serving: 900

Pan-Fried Noodles
Homemade fast food

Feeds 4:

1/2 pound egg noodles

Salt

1 pound boneless chicken breasts

1 bunch green onions

1 small piece fresh ginger (half-thumb sized)

2 cloves garlic

5-6 tablespoons vegetable or peanut oil

1/4-1/2 teaspoon red chile flakes

3 tablespoons soy sauce

1-2 tablespoons fresh lemon juice

1 Cook the noodles in 2 quarts of boiling, salted water (read the label on the package to see how long to cook the noodles). Don't let the noodles get too soft—they still have to be pan-fried. Pour them into a colander and drain well.

2 Cut the chicken into strips about as thick as your little finger. Wash the green onions, and cut off the green ends that look wilted. Remove the root ends and slice the rest of the onions into fine rings. Peel the ginger and garlic cloves, and chop them very finely.

3 Get a wok or large skillet really hot, then coat it with 3-4 tablespoons of the oil. Throw in the chicken, keep stirring vigorously, and fry for just 1-2 minutes. Push the chicken to one side of the pan, add a small amount of fresh oil to the middle of the pan, and stir-fry the onion, ginger, garlic, and chile flakes.

4 Add the last drops of the oil to the pan along with the noodles—don't stop stirring! After about 1 minute, sprinkle with the soy sauce and lemon juice—there'll be a nice loud hiss and delicious aromas will rise from the pan. Now: put that fork down and grab those chopsticks!

Prep time: 30 minutes
Good with: green tea, jasmine tea, or beer
Calories per serving: 630

43

Spaghetti Aglio Olio
Inexpensive, really simple, really quick

Feeds 4:

Salt

1 pound spaghetti

4 cloves garlic

3 tablespoons extra virgin olive oil

Freshly ground pepper

1 In a large pot, bring 5 quarts of water to a rolling boil and add 2 tablespoons salt. Toss in the spaghetti and cook until slightly firm to the bite—*al dente* (test it after 7-8 minutes).

2 Peel the garlic and cut it into fine slices. Pour the olive oil into a large skillet and heat slowly—don't let it get so hot that it hisses! Sauté the garlic gently in the hot oil.

3 Pour the spaghetti into a colander and let it drain. Add the spaghetti to the garlic mixture in the pan, and toss well. Season with salt and pepper.

Prep time: 20 minutes
Good with: French bread, arugula salad, Italian white wine
Calories per serving: 520

Spaghetti with Clams
Magnifico!
Needed: 2 huge pots

Feeds 4:

Salt

2 pounds fresh clams in their shells

1 large onion

3-4 cloves garlic

6 tablespoons olive oil

1/2 teaspoon red chile flakes

1 cup dry white wine

1 pound spaghetti

1/2 bunch fresh Italian parsley

Freshly ground pepper

1 In a large pot, bring 5 quarts of water and 2 tablespoons salt to a boil (for speed, use the highest heat with the lid on). Wash the clams with a small brush under cool running water and discard any opened ones. Peel the onion and garlic. Cut the onion in half, then cut it into thin strips. Chop the garlic.

2 Heat the olive oil in another large pot over medium heat. Toss in the onion, garlic, and chile flakes, stir, and sauté for 2 minutes. Add the clams and the wine—sniff—and cover the pot with the lid. The contents of pot shouldn't sizzle, just gently simmer for about 10 minutes.

3 Now it's spaghetti time: Drop the spaghetti into the boiling water and cook until slightly firm to the bite—*al dente* (test it after 7-8 minutes). Pour it into a colander and let drain.

4 Wash the parsley, shake it dry, and finely chop (hint: the bigger the knife, the easier it is to chop). Open the clam pot, and pick out and discard any unopened clams. Season with salt and pepper to taste, throw in the parsley, and that's it. Add the spaghetti and stir everything in the clam pot well. Get ready for a feast!

Prep time: 40 minutes
Good with: lots of crusty French bread to dip into the clam broth, white wine
Calories per serving: 670

Basic Tip

Spaghetti always tastes good, but try other pastas too. Most sauces go just as well with tagliatelle, or linguine, or penne, or rigatoni, or fusilli, or...(you get the idea).

Spaghetti with Tomato Sauce
A lifesaver when the stores are closed!

Feeds 4:

1 onion

2 cloves garlic

2-3 tablespoons olive oil

1 large can peeled tomatoes (28 ounces)

Salt

1 pound spaghetti

Freshly ground pepper

Red chile flakes, balsamic vinegar, red wine, chopped fresh Italian parsley (optional)

1 chunk Parmesan cheese (enough for this meal and then some)

1 Peel and mince both the onion and garlic. Heat the olive oil in a big skillet over medium heat and sauté the onion and garlic until translucent. Open the tomato can and chop up the tomatoes with a knife. Pour the tomatoes and juice into the skillet, add salt to taste, and simmer for at least 10 minutes—though longer won't hurt! Don't forget to stir periodically.

2 In a large pot, bring 5 quarts of water and 2 tablespoons salt to a rolling boil. Add the spaghetti and cook until it is slightly firm to the bite—*al dente*—don't forget to begin testing after 7-8 minutes!

3 Taste the sauce—anything missing? Probably salt and pepper (or you might add chile flakes, balsamic vinegar, red wine, or chopped fresh parsley to taste...the possibilities are endless)

4 Pour the cooked spaghetti in a colander and let it drain. Pour the hot spaghetti straight into the hot tomato sauce and toss. Have waiting on the table, as always, the Parmesan cheese and the grater.

Prep time: 30 minutes
Good with: French bread, green salad, wine
Calories per serving: 590

Spaghetti with Shrimp and Lemon Cream
Fast and elegant

Feeds 4:

4 green onions

1 teaspoon butter

Salt

1 pound spaghetti

1 cup heavy cream

1/2 cup vegetable stock

2-3 tablespoons fresh lemon juice

Freshly ground pepper

8 ounces small, peeled, cooked shrimp

A couple of fresh basil leaves

1 Wash the green onions, remove the root ends and wilted green parts, and chop the rest into very fine pieces. Melt the butter in a big skillet over medium heat and sauté the green onion until softened.

2 In a large pot, bring 5 quarts water and 2 tablespoons salt to a rolling boil. Drop in the spaghetti and cook until slightly firm to the bite—*al dente* (don't forget to test it after 7-8 minutes).

3 Pour the cream, vegetable stock, and lemon juice into the skillet, and simmer gently, stirring constantly. The liquid will gradually reduce, leaving a delicious creamy sauce (don't let the mixture come to a boil).

4 Taste-test the sauce, and season with salt and pepper. Right before serving, add the small peeled shrimp to the sauce; cook them only long enough to just heat through, otherwise they'll get tough. Drain the spaghetti in a colander, pour it straight into the skillet with the sauce, and toss well. Top with basil leaves, and serve hot.

Prep time: 30 minutes
Good with: French bread, white wine
Calories per serving: 670

Lasagna
Couch potatoes: better skip this one

Feeds 4-6:

1/4 cup butter (softened)

3 tablespoons flour

3 cups milk

1 bay leaf

1 small piece lemon zest

Salt, freshly ground pepper

Freshly ground nutmeg

1 onion

2 cloves garlic

1/4 cup olive oil

1 pound ground meat (or oyster mushrooms)

1 small can peeled tomatoes (14 ounces)

1/2 cup dry red wine

2 tablespoons butter

12 sheets green lasagna noodles (choose the precooked type)

4 ounces Romano cheese, freshly grated

1 Making lasagna teaches you one of life's basics—how to make the most important sauce of all, the sauce you remember from grandma's kitchen, the one with the funny name: béchamel—otherwise known as white sauce. In a saucepan, melt the butter slowly over *very* low heat, sprinkle in the flour, and stir briskly with a wooden spoon until the flour changes color just slightly, from white to pale yellow. Then, quickly pour in the milk, stirring constantly! Toss in the bay leaf and lemon zest for a hint of fresh flavor, and simmer gently for maybe 10 or 15 minutes—until the sauce starts to thicken slightly. Check on the sauce and stir with a whisk now and then. Finally, remove the lemon zest and bay leaf and season to taste with salt, pepper, and nutmeg.

2 Making lasagna teaches you a second of life's basics: how to make ragu—otherwise known as meat sauce. Though it's usually made from ground beef or veal, it's just as good with ground turkey or oyster mushrooms. First things first: peel and finely chop the onion and garlic. In a large skillet, heat the olive oil over medium heat and sauté the onion and garlic until translucent. Add the ground meat (or cleaned and finely chopped oyster mushrooms), mix well, and sauté until the meat is crumbly and no pink remains. Add the canned tomatoes (with the juice) and red wine, stir, and season with salt and pepper to taste. Now, cover the pan and

let the whole thing sit simmering for 15-20 minutes while you're working on the rest.

3 The rest of the preparation starts with preheating the oven to 400°F; set the oven shelf on the second level up from the bottom. What else? Find a dish for the lasagna. A lasagna dish is usually square or rectangular, and made from ceramic, glass, or metal (make sure it's ovenproof). Found one? OK, grease the inside with some of the soft butter.

4 Now comes the creative part—you're going to layer all the ingredients and have nothing leftover at the end. Start with some béchamel sauce, lay some lasagna noodles on top, then some ragu, more lasagna noodles and so on. You decide how many layers—just make sure that the top layer is the béchamel.

5 Now comes the easy part—stick the lasagna in the oven and kick back for 30 minutes. Then, sprinkle the cheese on top, dot with the rest of the butter, and after 10 minutes you'll blow your guests away with a luscious lasagna to die for. Let the lasagna stand for a few minutes on the countertop before cutting it into serving squares.

Prep time: actively cooking 1 hour, relaxing 40 minutes
Good with: a giant salad with lots of veggies
Calories per serving (6): 810

Tip: Lasagna noodles are very versatile. You can stuff or roll them; cut them up and boil them like noodles; and use them for all kinds of foods in the place of homemade pasta dough.

Potato Dumplings with Swiss Cheese
Really filling. And they won't break the bank

Feeds 4:

7 ounces good Swiss cheese

1 pound flour

4 eggs

Salt

1 cup lukewarm water

2 onions

2 tablespoons butter

Freshly ground pepper

1 Go ahead and grate the cheese right now—never keep a dumpling waiting once it's out of the water...

2 In a bowl, gently blend the flour, eggs, 1-2 teaspoons salt, and the water. Stir the mixture to make a smooth dough—it shouldn't be quite as thick as cake batter, yet not as runny as pancake batter—it should cling to a spoon.

3 Fill a big pot with 3 quarts of water, add 1 tablespoon salt, cover, and bring to a boil. Peel the onions and slice them into thin rings. Melt the butter in a small skillet over medium heat and sauté the onions till they're golden brown; keep warm. Preheat the oven to 400°F, and place a large ovenproof dish in the oven to warm.

4 The water must be boiling by now. So, whisk off the lid and put a spaetzle press (available in a specialty store) or dumpling maker—a plastic colander will do—on top of the pot. Add a good helping of dough and press it through the holes, using a wooden spoon to break off the dumplings. The strips of dough will plunge to the bottom of the pot at first—keep cooking them until they pop back up to the surface of the water. It takes about 3-5 minutes to cook each batch. Remove the dumplings on the surface of the water with a skimmer, drain well, and put them straight in the hot dish.

5 Repeat the cooking process with the next batch of dough. Sprinkle pepper and cheese on each layer of cooked dumplings. Sprinkle the top layer with the onions and hot butter, increase the oven heat to 425°F and bake for 5 minutes, until browned. Plan on not being hungry for a while after you eat these!

Prep time: 1 hour
Good with: tossed green salad
Calories per serving: 735

47

Simple Risotto
Impressive, and easier than you think!

What is it about Italian food that has us falling for it over and over again? One thing's for sure—in Italy you always find the most spectacular basics on the menu, like spaghetti and risotto. Anyone can make spaghetti, but mastering the art of risotto making takes real dedication.

Feeds 4 as part of a meal:

1 onion

1/4 cup butter

1½ cups Arborio rice

1/2 cup dry white wine

About 1 quart hot chicken, beef, or

vegetable stock

1/8-1/4 teaspoon crumbled saffron threads

2 ounces Parmesan cheese, freshly grated

Salt, freshly ground pepper

1 Even though your stirring finger may be itching, you must first peel and finely dice the onion. Then, melt 2 tablespoons of the butter in a saucepan and sauté the onion until it is translucent.

2 Pour the rice into the pan, and stir it into the buttery onions over really, really low heat, until it turns whitish and translucent—don't let it get brown. Pour in the wine and a ladle of hot stock and make sure you stir everything well.

3 Obviously the pan stays uncovered so that you can keep stirring while the rice is cooking. But there's another reason—the liquid isn't only absorbed by the rice, it also evaporates, and must be replaced with another ladleful of stock as the previous ladleful is absorbed.

4 While you're watching and stirring, you'll notice that everything suddenly gets nice and creamy. It'll look even better in a minute. Dissolve the saffron in the last of the stock, stir it into the pan, and the contents will be drenched in a rich deep-yellow color.

5 All in all, you've been standing at the stove for about 20-30 minutes and haven't been bored for a second. The first spoonful of risotto is for the cook; take a bite to test whether those soft-looking grains of rice still have a slightly firm center, indicating perfectly cooked risotto.

6 Stir the rest of the butter into the rice, add the fragrant fresh Parmesan, season with salt and pepper to taste, and you're good to go!

Prep time: 40 minutes
Good with: light white wine
Calories per serving: 390

Basic Tip

Once you've caught the risotto bug you can try a new one every day! How about one with green asparagus or cooked butternut squash? With fresh chanterelle mushrooms or dried porcini? With fresh spring peas or sautéed fennel? With cucumber or artichoke hearts? Or with ham or shrimp? The basic idea is always the same: sauté the vegetables in butter, stir the rice into the pan, and follow the above directions. The only difference is that if you want to add delicate ingredients like peas or meat or shrimp, which can't take long cooking, add them just before serving and cook for a few minutes only.

Paella
Perfect for parties—invite your guests to pitch in!

If you didn't haul a paella pan back with you from your sojourn to Spain, just use the biggest skillet you can lay your hands on.

Feeds 6:

6 small chicken thighs

1 pound fresh clams, mussels, or a combination

6 large shrimp, unpeeled

7 ounces firm sausage, such as chorizo, kielbasa, or garlic sausage

1 red bell pepper

1 green bell pepper

1 pound large, ripe tomatoes

1 large onion

3 cloves garlic

5 cups chicken or meat stock

8 tablespoons olive oil

Salt, freshly ground pepper

1 box frozen peas (10 ounces)

1 teaspoon sweet paprika

1/8-1/4 teaspoon crumbled saffron threads

1 pound Arborio rice

2 lemons

1 This one's high on ingredients, but low on stress. Wash the chicken thighs, shellfish (discard any open shells), and shrimp and pat dry with paper towels. Slice the sausage.

2 Wash the peppers, cut them in half, and remove the stems, seeds, and ribs. Cut the pepper halves into strips. Wash, core, and dice the tomatoes. Peel and mince the onion and garlic.

3 Heat the stock in a pot, throw in the shellfish, cover the pot, and cook over medium heat until the shells open (2-3 minutes). Transfer the shellfish to a plate and keep the stock hot. Discard any unopened shellfish shells.

4 Set the paella pan—or your giant skillet—over 2 burners, pour in the oil, and let it get really hot. Fry the chicken thighs in the oil over high heat for about 15 minutes, until golden brown on all sides. Transfer the chicken to a plate and season lightly with salt and pepper. Toss in the shrimp and cook for just 1-2 minutes, until they turn a nice pink color. Transfer the shrimp to a plate.

5 Stir the onion and garlic into the pan, add the pepper strips, tomatoes, and peas (straight from the freezer), and season with salt, pepper, and paprika to taste. Strain the hot stock through a sieve, then dissolve the saffron in the stock.

6 Don't forget the rice! Stir the rice into the pan well; then, pour the hot stock on top. Now let the whole shebang simmer for 15 minutes on the stovetop, until the rice absorbs most of the liquid. Five minutes after that, preheat the oven to 350°F.

7 Everything that isn't in the pan already now goes on the top: the chicken thighs, shellfish, shrimp, sausage—arrange it all decoratively on the rice. Put a large sheet of aluminum foil over the pan and seal the edges. Now the pan goes in the oven—and you've got 30 minutes to set the table, open the wine, cut the lemons into wedges and to look forward to dinner!

Prep time: a good 2 hours
Good with: a dry Spanish white wine
Calories per serving: 820

Nasi Goreng
Fried rice with a twist

This traditional Indonesian rice dish can be prepared with thousands of different ingredients—vegetables, fish, poultry, or meat—it's all good. And it's the very best way to use up yesterday's leftover rice.

Feeds 2:

1½ cups long-grain rice (or 3 cups leftover cooked rice)

2½ cups water (if using raw rice)

Salt

4 green onions

2 carrots

7 ounces Chinese cabbage

3½ ounces bean sprouts

2 cloves garlic

1 small piece fresh ginger (thumb-sized)

5 tablespoons vegetable oil

3 tablespoons soy sauce

1-2 teaspoons *sambal oelek*, or other hot chile paste

1-2 tablespoons fresh lemon juice

1 tablespoon ketchup

4 eggs

Freshly ground pepper

1 If you're using raw rice, rinse it well and put it in a saucepan with the water. Add a touch of salt, cover the pan, and turn the heat to high. As soon as the water starts to boil, turn down heat to very low, place the lid on the pan, and let the rice absorb the liquid for 15-20 minutes. Remove the pan from the stove, and let the rice stand with the lid on. Or, bring the leftover rice to room temperature.

2 Wash and trim the green onions, and peel the carrots. Wash the Chinese cabbage, and cut away the coarse stems. Chop all of the vegetables into thin strips. Give the sprouts a quick rinse, and let them drain. Peel and finely slice the garlic and ginger.

3 Heat 4 tablespoons of the oil in a wok or large skillet. Place the garlic, ginger, and all the veggies—except the sprouts—in the pan. Using a spatula, stir-fry the mixture for 2 minutes. Now, add the rice and stir-fry for 2 more minutes. Season with the soy sauce, *sambal oelek*, lemon juice and ketchup, mix in the sprouts, and stir-fry for 2-3 more minutes.

4 Here's the challenge, Indonesian style: While you're doing all this, have a second skillet going, heat the rest of the oil, and fry the 4 eggs. Season them with salt and pepper to taste.

5 Serve the rice mixture on plates and perch a fried egg on top of each portion. (Though you'll feel like using chopsticks for this one, it's really much easier to eat with a fork.)

Prep time: 45 minutes
Good with: cucumber salad, Asian beer
Calories per serving: 640

Lemony Rice Pilaf
Goes with anything!

Feeds 4 as a side dish:

1½ cups long-grain rice

1 onion

2-3 tablespoons butter

2½ cups chicken stock

Salt, freshly ground pepper

1/2 teaspoon grated lemon zest

1 Put the rice in a sieve and rinse it under cold water until the water runs clear; drain. Peel and finely chop the onion. In a saucepan, melt half of the butter over medium heat and sauté the onion until it turns translucent. Pour in the stock and bring to a boil.

2 Now it's time to add the rice and season with a touch of salt and pepper. Reduce the heat to very low, cover the pan, and wait for about 20 minutes—resist the urge to stir!

3 When all the liquid has been absorbed, remove the pan from the stove. Drape a kitchen towel between the pan and the lid and let stand for 10 minutes. Fluff the rice with a fork and stir in rest of the butter and the lemon zest.

Prep time: 45 minutes
Good with: just about everything—from grilled fish to vegetable stew
Calories per serving: 130

Pancakes
Not just for breakfast anymore

There's one thing to remember about these pancakes—they've got to be thin. Why? Because you're going to want to roll them up and stick them straight into your mouth—or stuff them with all kinds of goodies.

Feeds 2-4:

1 cup flour

1/2 cup milk

4 eggs

Pinch of salt

2 tablespoons vegetable oil

1 Place the flour in a bowl. Using a whisk, gradually blend in the milk, eggs, and salt. The batter should be thick and smooth, without any little lumps. Let the batter stand for 20 minutes.

2 Coat the bottom of a skillet with a tiny bit of oil (or clarified butter) and get it hot, then turn heat down to medium. Ladle about 1/4 cup of the batter into the pan and quickly swirl it so that the batter is distributed in a thin, even coat.

3 When the pancake is brown underneath, shake the pan to jog it loose. Then, using a spatula, flip it over (or toss it in the air if you feel like showing off) and brown the other side. Remove the pancake from the pan.

4 Coat the skillet with a tiny drop of oil again and ladle in another batch of batter; cook it in the same way. Each pancake takes just a couple of minutes, but if you wait until the last one's finally ready, the first one will be sitting cold and forlorn on the plate. So it's best to serve the pancakes as you go—or keep them warm in a preheated 350°F oven.

Prep time: 1 hour
Good with: salad, mushroom sauce, meat sauce, and all kinds of vegetable stews.
Try this good, fast treat: top the pancakes with cheese while they are still in the skillet, roll them up, and let the cheese melt for a while. Another tip: spread the pancakes with something sweet, like fruit puree, compote, or jam, or even top with fruit salad.
Calories per serving (4): 270

Veggie Frittata
Italian-style omelet

Feeds 4 as an appetizer:

9 ounces small, firm zucchini (or another favorite veggie)

1 small onion

2 cloves garlic

1/4 cup olive oil

Salt, freshly ground pepper

1 bunch fresh chives

5 eggs

5 tablespoons milk

1 Wash the zucchini, trim the ends, and slice thinly; then, cut the slices into matchstick strips. Peel and mince the onion and garlic. Heat the olive oil in a nonstick skillet over medium heat. Add the zucchini, onion, and garlic, and sauté until the vegetables are tender. Season to taste with salt and pepper.

2 Wash, shake dry, and finely chop the chives. Whisk the eggs with the milk, and season lightly with salt and pepper. Add half of the chives to the egg-milk mixture and pour over the zucchini. Lift the pan and swirl the mixture so that it spreads out evenly in the pan. Cook over low heat until the eggs are set.

3 Invert the frittata onto a plate—or an upside-down lid—and slide it back into the skillet to brown the other side, about 5 more minutes. Cut into wedges to serve.

Prep time: 30 minutes
Good with: grated cheese, fresh tomato sauce, salad
Calories per serving: 210

Potato "Tortilla"
Spanish-style omelet

Feeds 4 as an appetizer:

2 large boiling potatoes (about 10 ounces)

1 onion

6-8 tablespoons olive oil

8 eggs

1/2 cup milk

1/2 cup heavy cream

Salt, freshly ground pepper

1/2 bunch fresh Italian parsley

Dry sherry (optional)

1 Wash and peel the potatoes. To dice them, first cut them into thick slices, then into thick strips, then into cubes. Peel and finely chop the onion.

2 Heat the oil in a skillet (make sure it has a lid that fits). Sauté the diced potatoes in the oil over medium heat for 10 minutes, stirring occasionally. Add the onion and sauté with the potatoes for 5 minutes.

3 Whisk the eggs with the milk and cream, and season well with salt and pepper. Wash the parsley, shake dry, chop, add it to the pan, and mix well.

4 Pour the egg mixture over the potatoes in the skillet. Cook slowly over low heat until the underside is set. Slide the tortilla out of the pan onto a plate—or an upside-down lid—and slide it back into the pan again, cooked-side up. Cover. The tortilla will be ready in about 5 minutes.

5 Serve the tortilla warm, right away. Or, allow it to cool, cut it into slices, and serve as tapas with little glasses of sherry as accompaniments.

Prep time: 45 minutes
Good with: marinated olives
Calories per serving: 430

Basic Tips

Tip #1: Replace half of the milk with sparkling water, to give the batter an especially light consistency.

Tip #2: To turn the pancakes over, try throwing them in one smooth movement in the direction of the ceiling, then catch them in the pan on the way down.

Mashed Potatoes
Pure Pleasure

Raise your hand if you remember what really good homemade mashed potatoes taste like. Of course, everyone does. And who knows how to make them? Not so many hands up this time. Here's how:

Feeds 4 as a side dish:

1½ pounds baking potatoes

1 tablespoon salt

1 onion (optional)

1/4 cup butter

1/2-1 cup milk

Freshly ground nutmeg

1 Wash, peel, and halve the potatoes. If they're big suckers, quarter them. Place the potato pieces in a saucepan and cover with salted water. Cover the pan and bring the water quickly to a boil; cook the potatoes for a good 15-20 minutes over medium heat, until they're tender.

2 Meanwhile, peel the onion (if using), cut it in half, and then into thin strips. Melt the butter in a skillet and brown the onion in the butter over medium heat.

3 Heat the milk in a saucepan; keep it warm, but do not let it boil. Drain the water off the potatoes and let them stand in the pot without a lid for 1 minute. Then, mash the potato pieces well with a potato masher or large fork, or push them through a potato ricer back into the pot.

4 Now, pour the hot milk over the potatoes and stir well—with a spoon to start, then with a whisk to fluff them. Add the fresh nutmeg to taste and mix well.

5 Now it's up to you: stir the butter and onions into the mashed potatoes, or serve them on top. Here's another idea: pour the mixture through a sieve and stir the flavored butter into the potatoes; scatter the onions over the top. For pure potato flavor, omit the onions and top the potatoes with pats of the butter. Food doesn't get any better than this!

Prep time: 30 minutes
Good with: everything—or nothing!
Calories per serving: 250

Basic Tip

So good and yet so cold—a common pitfall when making mashed potatoes. If you want to serve warm mashed potatoes, make sure that all the ingredients— potatoes, milk, onions—are as hot as possible when they are combined. Then, set the potatoes on the stove over very low heat—they'll not only get warmer, but also get fluffier. To keep the potatoes warm, set the pot on top of another same-sized pot of boiling water until you're ready for them.

Potatoes Boiled in their Jackets
Very basic, very good

In England, potatoes cooked in their skins are called "jacket potatoes." They're common in British pubs, where they're served with a variety of savory toppings.

Feeds 4 as a snack:

2¼ pounds same-sized boiling potatoes

Salt

1 tub sour cream (16 ounces)

Freshly ground pepper

1 bunch fresh chives (or other fresh herbs)

About 2 tablespoons prepared horseradish

1/2 cup butter

1 Wash the potatoes under running water, scrubbing hard with a brush so that the skin is really clean—then you can eat the skin along with the potatoes.

2 Put the potatoes in a saucepan and add water, just enough to cover the potatoes, and throw in 1 teaspoon salt. Cover the pan, bring the water to a boil, then simmer the potatoes over low heat for about 15-20 minutes (the cooking time depends on the size of the potatoes). Poke the spuds with a fork or small sharp knife to see whether they are getting soft.

3 While the potatoes are cooking, blend the sour cream with salt and pepper to taste. Wash, shake dry, and chop the herbs, then mix them into the sour cream.

4 Now, pour the water out of the pan—keeping the potatoes from falling out. Use oven mitts or an oven cloth to grip the hot pan tightly, slide the lid off a tad, and carefully pour off the water. Let the potatoes stand in the uncovered pan for a while to drive off some of the steam.

5 Serve the potatoes nice and hot, with the peel on. It's best to cover them with a cloth so they don't cool down very fast. Eat them with the herbed sour cream, horseradish, butter, and salt.

Prep time: 45 minutes
Good with: smoked salmon, your favorite sauces and dips, such as Creamy Green Sauce (p 88), Tzatziki (p 90), Tuna Dip (p 91), or Ratatouille (p 144)
Calories per serving: 630

Baked Potatoes
Virtually stress-free

Feeds 4 as a side dish:

8 large baking potatoes (each about 5-7 ounces)

Caraway seeds (optional)

Coriander seeds (optional)

Coarsely ground pepper (optional)

Dried herbs, such as marjoram, thyme, oregano, rosemary (optional)

1 Preheat the oven to 450°F. Set the oven rack in the middle of the oven.

2 Wash the potatoes, prick them all over with a fork, and wrap each one in foil together with caraway seeds, coriander, pepper, or herbs to taste.

3 Set the foil-wrapped potatoes on the oven rack and bake for about 1 hour (depending on size). Prick with a skewer or knife to test for doneness. Let stand for a few minutes before serving.

Prep time: 1¼ hours
Good with: fresh butter, sour cream, herbed cream cheese, steak, and salad
Calories per serving: 210

Pan-Fried potatoes
(AKA Cottage Fries)

Feeds 4 as a side dish:
Cottage fries: Take one!

1¾ pounds Yukon gold potatoes

Salt

4-6 tablespoons vegetable oil

Freshly ground pepper

1 Wash the potatoes. Place them in a saucepan, cover with salted water, and bring to a boil. Reduce the heat and simmer until the potatoes are slightly underdone. Pour off the water and let the potatoes cool (preferably overnight, refrigerated). Then, peel the potatoes and cut into thin slices.

2 In a cast-iron skillet (or uncoated stainless-steel skillet), heat half of the oil over medium heat. Distribute the potato slices in the pan—it's best if they're not overlapping. Cook them without disturbing them for 10 minutes. Then, season with salt and pepper, turn each potato slice, and sauté for another 5-8 minutes in the rest of the oil until they're tender inside and crispy outside.

Cottage fries: Take two!

1¾ pounds Yukon gold potatoes

6 tablespoons olive oil (nothing fancy)

2 tablespoons butter

Salt, freshly ground pepper

1 Wash, peel, and cube the potatoes. Heat the oil in a large skillet (with a lid that fits), add the diced potatoes, toss them in the oil, and sauté for a couple of minutes.

2 Put the lid on the pan and cook the potatoes over medium heat for 10-15 minutes, until golden brown. Off with the lid, in with the butter, and cook for 5-10 more minutes, turning occasionally, until the potatoes are crispy. Season well with salt and pepper.

Prep time:
#1: 1 hour (plus cooling time)
#2: 40 minutes
Good with: anything from fried eggs to roast pork, to smoked salmon, to ratatouille
Calories per serving:
#1: 210
#2: 270

Potatoes Au Gratin
Impress your friends!

Feeds 4 as a side dish:

1/2 cup heavy cream

1/2 cup milk

Generous 1 pound baking potatoes

1 tablespoon butter

Freshly ground nutmeg

Salt, freshly ground pepper

2 ounces Swiss cheese, grated

1 Stir the cream and milk together. Wash and peel the potatoes, and cut away any dark or green spots. Thinly slice the potatoes. Preheat the oven to 350°F.

2 Smear an ovenproof dish with a bit of the butter. Arrange the potato slices in rows in the dish so that the slices overlap. Sprinkle each layer with a little nutmeg and season lightly with salt and pepper. Pour the milk-cream mixture into the dish, sprinkle the cheese over the top, and dot with the rest of the butter. Bake in the oven for about 50 minutes, until the potatoes are soft and browned. Let them stand for a few minutes before serving.

Prep time: 1 hour
Good with: chicken, steak, or a great salad!
Calories per serving: 245

German Potato Dumplings
Homemade, naturally

Feeds 4 as a side dish:

2 pounds baking potatoes

1/2-1 cup flour

Salt

Freshly ground nutmeg

2 eggs

2-3 tablespoons butter

1/4 cup coarse bread crumbs

1 If you have such a thing as a potato ricer in your kitchen, go straight to next step! If not, read on. Wash the potatoes, place them in a saucepan, and cover with water (barely). Boil the potatoes until tender, about 20-30 minutes, depending on size. Drain and refrigerate overnight. Peel the cold potatoes and coarsely grate them. (Proceed to step 3!)

2 If you are the lucky owner of a potato ricer, wash the potatoes, place them in a saucepan, and cover with water (barely). Boil the potatoes until tender, about 20-30 minutes, depending on size. Pour off the water, let stand a while to drive off the steam, and carefully peel the hot potatoes (use a paring knife). Force the hot potatoes through the ricer right away and fluff up the potato mush so it doesn't clump together.

3 Sprinkle about 2/3 of the flour over the potatoes and season to taste with salt and nutmeg. Then, break the eggs into a small bowl and beat with a fork. Use the fork to fold the eggs into the potato dough. Now, knead all ingredients with your hands to a smooth dough as quickly as possible. If the dough doesn't want to bind, add more flour. Don't over-knead, or the dough will be too soft and take on too much flour.

4 Next, dust your hands lightly with flour and separate the dough into small portions. Using your fingers, make a little ball with each portion of dough.

5 Meanwhile, bring a big pot of salted water to a boil. Drop the dumplings in the water, cover the pot, and bring to boil again. Then, let the dumplings cook with the lid half off for 10-20 minutes, until all of the dumplings bob to the surface of the water.

6 Melt the butter in a small skillet, stir in the bread crumbs, and sauté until toasty and brown. Remove the dumplings from the water with a skimmer, let the water drip off, place on a serving plate, and pour the buttered bread crumbs over the top.

Prep time: 1½ hours
Good with: lots of sauce, roasts, stews, poultry, vegetables, mushrooms
Calories per serving: 400

Basic Tips
Gnocchi—Italian potato dumplings
Here's what you do: follow the recipe on the left, but roll out long strips of dough and cut them into bite-sized pieces. Then, use a fork to make ridges in each piece—this will help the sauce cling. Now they're ready for the pot! When cooked, toss them briefly in hot butter and sage leaves (see photo above) or your favorite sauce.

Potato Fritters
Peel some potatoes—they must be the baking type—and grate them, but not too finely. Roll the grated potatoes briefly in a paper towel to dry. Season with salt and pepper, then divide into small portions. Using a spoon, place the potato portions in hot oil, pat into smooth patties, and fry until crispy and brown. Enjoy the fritters hot with applesauce or sauerkraut, German style!

Spinach-Cheese Dumplings
Make them with a friend

Feeds 4:

1 tablespoon butter

1 box frozen spinach (10 ounces), thawed

5 ounces ricotta cheese

4 ounces Parmesan cheese, freshly grated

2 eggs

1 egg yolk

Salt, freshly ground pepper

Freshly ground nutmeg

About 1¼ cups flour

1 Grease an ovenproof baking dish with the butter. Finely chop the thawed spinach, and place in a bowl with the ricotta. Stir in half of the Parmesan, the eggs, and egg yolk. Season with salt, pepper, and nutmeg. Spoon in the flour. Using a whisk or hand mixer, stir until a smooth dough forms. Add a bit more flour if needed.

2 In a big pot, bring 3 quarts of salted water to a boil. Preheat the oven to 350°F. When the water boils, make dumplings from the dough: using a tablespoon, cut off one mini-portion of dough at a time. With another spoon, pat the dumpling smooth and flip it into the boiling water.

3 Let the dumplings cook for a few minutes over low heat. When the dumplings are ready, they will bob to the surface of the water. Fish them out with a skimmer, drain, and place them in the buttered baking dish. Scatter the rest of the Parmesan over the dumplings and bake for 5 minutes, until the top is golden brown.

Prep time: 1 hour
Good with: French bread, green salad, dry white wine
Calories per serving: 420

French Fries
There's definitely an art to them

Feeds 4 as a snack:

1¼ pounds russet potatoes

Salt

Peanut or vegetable oil

Ketchup (very American), malt vinegar (very British), or homemade mayo (very Belgian) for dipping

1 Wash and peel the potatoes, and cut them into chunky strips. Rinse off the surface starch in cold water. Dry the potatoes well.

2 Half-fill a large, deep-sided skillet (or deep-fat fryer if you have one) with oil and heat the oil until it's really hot. Test the heat with a cube of bread—it should sizzle as soon as it touches the oil.

3 Important: pre-fry potatoes in small batches just for 2-3 minutes; remove them from the oil before they color, and drain on paper towels (it's OK if they cool down). If too many potatoes go into the pan at once, the oil quickly cools down and is soaked up by the potatoes.

4 Dunk the pre-fried potatoes into the hot oil a second time—this time they can practically all go in together. Fry for 4-5 minutes, so that they turn crispy and golden brown. Drain the potatoes well, sprinkle generously with salt, and enjoy with your favorite dipping sauce.

Prep time: 45 minutes
Good with: whatever!!
Calories per serving: 440

59

Pizza
Child's play

There's an old wives' tale that making yeast dough is complicated, boring, and often goes wrong. Trust us—it's just a myth!!

Feeds 4:
Pizza dough:
1 package fast-acting yeast

2 cups flour

1/4 cup olive oil

1/2 cup lukewarm water

1 generous pinch salt

Tomato sauce:
1 onion

2 cloves garlic

1 tablespoon olive oil

1 large can peeled tomatoes (28 ounces)

Salt, freshly ground pepper

Your choice:
Sliced mozzarella, basil, pitted olives, anchovies, capers, ham, artichoke hearts, fresh mushrooms, salami, pepperoni, tuna, bell peppers, onions, goat cheese, arugula, nuts...the sky's the limit!

1-2 tablespoons olive oil to drizzle over the top

1 It doesn't get any easier than this—in a bowl, mix the yeast with the flour. Add the oil and water and mix well. Stir in the salt. Work the mixture wtih your hands to make a smooth dough. Cover the bowl with a cloth, and let the dough rise for about 45 minutes, until it has doubled in volume. That's it!

2 While the dough is rising, prepare the tomato sauce and everything else that's going to go on top of the pizza.

3 Peel the onion and garlic and chop finely. In a skillet, heat the olive oil over medium heat, and sauté the onion and garlic until translucent. Chop the tomatoes into small pieces and stir into the skillet. Let the sauce simmer gently, uncovered, over medium heat for a few minutes, until slightly thickened. Taste and season with salt and pepper.

4 Preheat the oven to 475°F. Grease a baking sheet. Remove the dough from the bowl and knead vigorously with your hands on a flour-dusted work surface. With a rolling pin, roll out the dough so it's large enough to cover the baking sheet. Carefully transfer the dough to the pan, and fold over the edges slightly to make a crust.

5 Spread the tomato sauce over the dough. Let everyone pick a section of the pizza and put on his or her own toppings. Drizzle olive oil over the whole pizza and bake for 15-20 minutes, until the cheese is melted and the crust is golden brown. Cut into squares.

Prep time: 1½ hours
Good with: green salad, Italian red wine
Calories per serving: 410

Ham 'n' Cheese Quiche
Freezes well for emergency rations

Feeds 4-6:

1¾ cups flour

1/2 teaspoon salt

2-3 tablespoons ice water

4 ounces cold butter

7 ounces cooked ham

1 onion

2 cloves garlic

5 ounces Swiss cheese (such as Gruyère or Emmentaler)

1 cup heavy cream

4 eggs

Freshly ground pepper

1 bunch fresh chives, or 1/2 bunch fresh Italian parsley

1 Pile the flour on a work surface, add the salt, and make a depression in the middle. Add 2-3 tablespoons of really cold water. Distribute the butter in little pieces around the edge of the flour; then, using a large knife, cut it into the mixture until the flour and butter bind to make a crumbly mixture. With your hands, knead the mixture just enough to make a smooth dough. Wrap the dough with plastic wrap and chill in the refrigerator for 30 minutes.

2 Now you've got time to cut the ham into strips, peel and chop the onion and garlic, and grate the cheese. And a minute or two to beat together the cream, eggs, and pepper, and to finely chop the herbs.

3 But don't forget the oven: preheat it to 425°F.

4 On a flour-dusted work surface, roll the dough with a rolling pin into a circle about 11 inches in diameter. Carefully transfer the dough to a 10-inch quiche dish (a fluted glass pie pan) and cut off any dough hanging over the edge of the dish.

5 In a bowl, mix the ham with the onion, garlic, and herbs, and distribute on top of the dough. Stir the cheese into the egg mixture, and pour on top of the ham mixture. Bake the quiche for about 40 minutes, until the eggs are set and the top and crust are golden brown. After about 20 minutes, cover the quiche with aluminum foil (shiny-side in) to prevent over-browning.

Prep time: 1 hour making it, 40 minutes baking it
Good with: green salad
Calories per serving (6): 685

Bruschetta
Good tomatoes + good
oil = good bruschetta

Feeds 4 as an appetizer:

4 ripe tomatoes

8 fresh basil leaves

4 large slices Italian or sourdough bread

4 cloves garlic

1/2 cup extra virgin olive oil

Salt, freshly ground pepper

1 Wash the tomatoes, cut out the green stems and cores, and cut into very small cubes. Chop the basil leaves into fine strips.

2 Cut the bread in half and toast in a toaster or hot oven until golden brown and crisp.

3 Peel and halve the garlic cloves. Rub the cloves generously onto one side of the toasted bread, and drizzle each slice with 1 tablespoon olive oil. Top each bread slice with the diced tomatoes, dividing evenly, and season with salt and pepper. Garnish with the basil strips.

Prep time: 20 minutes
Good with: white wine
Calories per serving: 275

Crostini with Olive Paste
A must-try!

This is the world's best olive paste, discovered by our friend Cornelia.

Feeds 4 as an appetizer:

4 ounces pitted kalamata olives

1 tablespoon capers

1 tablespoon pine nuts

2 tablespoons tomato paste

2 tablespoons olive oil

1 teaspoon balsamic vinegar

Freshly ground pepper

12 thin slices baguette, Italian white bread, ciabatta, or Melba toast

1 Finely puree the olives with the capers, pine nuts, tomato paste, and oil. Season with the balsamic vinegar and pepper (there's no need for salt—olives are salty enough).

2 Toast the bread slices in a toaster or very hot oven until golden brown and crisp. Spread the bread with the olive paste and eat right away!

Prep time: 10 minutes
Good with: any apéritif
Calories per serving: 235

Olga's Canapés
Guaranteed to impress

Our Russian friend, Olga, always serves these snacks when there's something important to celebrate.

Feeds 4 as an appetizer:

1 cup crème fraîche

3/4 cup sour cream

1 baguette

1 bunch fresh chives

2 ounces black caviar (use genuine sturgeon eggs—incredibly expensive—or a less expensive type—your choice)

2 ounces red caviar (salmon or trout)

1 In a bowl, stir the crème fraîche with the sour cream until smooth. Cut the baguette into thin slices. Wash the chives and chop them finely.

2 Spread the creamy mixture onto the bread, pile the black and red caviar on top, and garnish with the chives.

Prep time: 15 minutes
Good with: Champagne, of course, or vodka served in tiny coffee cups
Calories per serving: 540

Savory Filled Croissants

Here are some seriously delicious ideas for stuffing croissants...Or make up your own!

Feeds 4:

1 sheet frozen puff pastry (1/2 of a 17.3-ounce box)

Salt, freshly ground pepper

1 egg

Ideas for fillings:

3½ ounces small white mushrooms

1 tablespoon fresh lemon juice

2 ounces Swiss cheese, grated

2 tablespoons chopped fresh Italian parsley

or:

6 ounces cooked ham

2½ ounces Swiss cheese, grated

2-3 tablespoons sour cream

1 tablespoon sharp mustard

Sweet paprika

1 Follow the instructions on the package for thawing the puff pastry. With a rolling pin, roll out the pastry slightly, so that you end up with a large square. Cut the pastry diagonally into fourths, so that you end up with 4 triangles. Preheat the oven to 350°F.

2 For the mushroom filling: wipe the mushrooms clean. Finely chop them, place in a bowl, and drizzle with the lemon juice. Season with salt and pepper. Mix in the grated cheese and chopped parsley.

3 For the ham filling: chop the ham into thin strips and place in a bowl. Mix in the cheese, sour cream, and mustard, and season to taste with salt, pepper, and paprika.

4 Separate the egg, place the white and yolk in separate bowls, and beat each slightly. Coat the edges of the pastry triangles with egg white (this holds the croissant together). Spread the filling over the pastry and roll up, starting from the straight sides of the triangles. Brush the tops with the egg yolk. Poke each croissant with a fork so that steam can escape while baking.

5 Rinse a baking sheet under cold water. Set the croissants on the tray, bending them slightly to resemble a crescent shape, and put the tray into the oven. After about 20-30 minutes, they should be crisp and brown.

Prep time: 50 minutes
Good with: green salad
Calories per serving:
Mushroom-360/Ham-430

Stuffed Baguette
Small on effort, big on taste

Feeds 4 as a snack:

2 cloves garlic

Fresh basil leaves

1/4 cup soft butter

10 ounces mozzarella cheese

4 medium-sized ripe tomatoes

1 baguette

Salt, freshly ground pepper

1 Preheat the oven to 400°F. Peel and finely chop the garlic, and cut the basil leaves into thin strips. Mix both with the soft butter. Cut the mozzarella into thin slices, and wash and slice the tomatoes.

2 Make deep cuts in the baguette at 1-inch intervals—do not cut all the way through. Spread each pocket with the seasoned butter, slide a mozzarella slice and a tomato slice into each one, and season with salt and pepper. Bake for 15 minutes, until the cheese is melted.

Prep time: 30 minutes
Good with: red wine
Calories per serving: 490

Salad
& Sou

Have an eye for detail? Know what's important? Chances are you can really cook!

s

p s

People who make good salads have an eye for detail. For example, they make sure the leafy ingredients are bite-sized, that the chunks of tomato are ripe, and they use a dressing that complements the salad ingredients. Then, everything gets tossed together—early enough for the salad's flavors to blend, but not so early that the ingredients turn to mush.

People who make good soup know what's important. Before they get down to work, good soup makers think about how they want the final product to be, and what has to go into the pot when.

If you have an eye for detail and know what's important, chances are you can really cook!

You can tell the people who just can't cook because they make bad salads and soups. Sorry, but that's how it is...

The good news is that if you pay attention, and if you're willing to learn, it's really easy to make good salads and soups.

And if you master making these well, the possibilities are endless....

Our favorite ingredient

The Onion

French: oignon; Italian: cipolla; Spanish: cebolla

Onions are:
• Brown, white, red, yellow, and green, and vary widely in size and flavor—from small and pungent, to big-as-your-fist and subtle
• aromatic and bold flavored (white and brown onions)
• sweet and fragrant (red onions)
• elegant and delicately flavored (shallots)
• long, lean, and fresh tasting (leeks and green onions)

Onions have:
• 60 calories per medium onion
• 14 g carbohydrates
• negligible fat
• lots of potassium and vitamin C

Onions can:
• clean out the airways
• get the digestion going
• cleanse the blood
• bring tears to your eyes

Onions need:
• to be stored in a cool, dark, and completely dry place
• to be alone—always—or something stored next to them will soon taste like onion
• to be cut only as needed (whenever possible) or they'll get bitter
• to sit only briefly in the salad, or their flavor will become too strong

Onions love:
• sautéing and frying—it makes them mellow and crispy
• slow braising—it makes them sweet, succulent, and tender
• powerful partners to complement their assertive nature, such as spicy, sour, smoky, or fatty flavors
• subtle companions to contrast with their bold qualities, such as sweet or creamy-textured ingredients

Vegetable Stock

Good stock is a must for good soup

Vegetable stock is a great all-purpose ingredient, since it tastes relatively neutral. And it's easy to make at home. Just wash some of your favorite veggies, trim them, and throw them all in a pot with your favorite spices, herbs, and a pinch of salt. Cover the contents with water two fingers deep, slowly bring to a boil, and simmer for 30-60 minutes—the timing depends on the vegetables. More tender herbs go into the stockpot (stalk and all) for the last 15 minutes. The last step is to pour the stock through a sieve, and taste.

Good vegetables for stock: Onions, tomatoes (for taste and color), leeks, celery, carrots, mushrooms, bell peppers, and fennel (lends a special flavor). Avoid potatoes and strong-tasting veggies like cabbage and broccoli.

Good spices and herbs for stock: Peppercorns, nutmeg, juniper berries, cloves (sparingly), bay leaves, rosemary, thyme, savory, chives, parsley, tarragon, basil (goes in right at the end). Use ginger, cinnamon, fennel, saffron, and caraway seeds for special dishes that need distinctive flavor.

Getting the Flavor Right

All salads—from pasta to tossed green—need to marinate for a little while in order to achieve the correct flavor balance. Is there anything worse than flavorless pasta salad? How about mushy, over-dressed green salad? But how do you know how long to marinate?

Ideal marinating times for salads, at a glance:

1 minute	tender salad greens (such as butter lettuce, leaf lettuce, arugula) are best eaten when absolutely fresh
up to 5 minutes	hardy salad greens (such as romaine lettuce, radicchio, endive, frisée, cabbage) can stand a little longer soak
15 minutes	tomato salad, cold potato salad
overnight	seafood salad
whole day	rice salad

Vinegar

Q: How is vinegar made?
A: Just open some wine—then forget about it.

Sooner or later it'll turn sour. There's always some bacteria flying around in the air just waiting to pounce on an open bottle of alcohol and convert it into acetic acid—otherwise known as vinegar. Vinegar gets its distinctive taste and name from the alcohol used to make it. An opened bottle of Chardonnay will become white wine vinegar. A forgotten, half-drunk bottle of Champagne will turn into Champagne vinegar. But to make high-quality vinegars, such as balsamic vinegar, you really have to know what you're doing—it takes years to mature and the method is quite complex.

Common types of vinegar: sherry vinegar, cider vinegar, raspberry vinegar, tarragon and other herb vinegars, malt vinegar (very British), beer vinegar (very German), and rice vinegar (very Asian).

Oil

Q: Where does oil come from?
A: It's extracted from plant sources.

The oil we use to cook with is obtained from oil-bearing fruits and seeds. We're talking humongous pressure here—so inside the press it gets quite hot. A solvent is sometimes added so the very last drops can be squeezed out. Once the solvent has been removed again, along with all the murky solids, you're left with refined oil. It's great for frying, and tastes very neutral. This is just what you want for salads that are piggybacks for other flavors. Some oils are made with a "cold press" method (at a temperature of less than 140°F). These have no added solvents and have not been refined—so they have the fullest flavor and retain their own natural taste. Some oils have unique flavors— if in doubt about how well its flavors will blend, try it first. Incidentally, olive oil labeled "extra virgin" is always cold pressed.

Common types of oil: sunflower, corn, and canola (these are mostly refined, and often blended and sold as vegetable oil or salad oil); olive oil (sold in many varieties, from extra virgin to pure to pomace); pumpkin seed oil, sesame oil, and various nut oils (very aromatic, often too strong by themselves—mix with a neutral oil to mellow the flavor.)

Salt

Q: Where do we get salt from?
A: All salt comes from the sea—honest!

Even in places where miners now hammer away at the rock-salt face, there was once an ocean. Over time the waters evaporated, leaving behind salt deposits; then, other rock was deposited on top. Today, this same salt reappears at the earth's surface dissolved in water that is pumped down into the earth by salt "manufacturers." The salty water is extracted, and evaporated again, usually with the aid of pressure and steam. In the case of "sea salt," there's been no long geological detour over millions of years. To harvest sea salt, seawater is diverted into special seabeds—also called pans—where it ends up evaporating (of course) and leaving behind solid rocks of salt crystals. It has to be purified before human consumption, yet even after all that, it still tastes more than just salty—it tastes like ocean. Some manufacturers add iodine to their salt, which stops our thyroid glands from going into overdrive and causing health problems.

In
Variations on the classic vinaigrette: with lemon, cheese, or soy sauce • a pantry well stocked with oils and vinegars • fresh herbs • plenty of homemade stock in the freezer • Caesar salad topped with chicken, steak, or salmon strips • pre-warmed soup plates • serving soup from a tureen • vegetable stew with curry and coconut milk • *never out of style: balsamic vinaigrette, soup for breakfast*

Out
Waterlogged salad and dressing • stale oil in the cruet • dried parsley and chives • big salad leaves that don't fit in your mouth • alcohol in the dressing • spectacular soup, but not enough for second helpings • soup that's all cream and no substance • serving stew in coffee mugs • noodles in cream soups • *never fashionable: oily salads, lukewarm soups*

Baby Greens Salad with Bacon and Mushrooms

Revealed: The secret to cleaning mushrooms—share it only with your closest friends!

Feeds 4 as an appetizer:

6 ounces smoked slab bacon

8 ounces baby salad greens

10 ounces small white mushrooms

4-5 tablespoons vegetable oil

Salt, freshly ground pepper

1 shot dry white wine (or sherry, or brandy, or balsamic vinegar)

1-2 tablespoons red wine vinegar

1 Remove and discard the rind from the bacon and cut the rest into small cubes. Sauté the bacon in a skillet (no oil) over medium heat, until crisp.

2 Wash the salad greens in lots of water—2-3 times if possible—so you don't wind up with grains of sand between your teeth. Snap off any coarse stems. Place the greens in a colander, drain, and dry well.

3 OK—now for the secret about mushrooms: never wash them—they'll get waterlogged and lose a lot of flavor. Just wipe the caps clean with a damp towel and cut off their dirty little feet. Quarter or halve the caps.

4 Get 2 tablespoons of the oil very hot in a large skillet that has a good lid. Throw in the mushrooms, toss them in the oil, and season to taste with salt and pepper. Then, pour in the wine (be generous) and cover the pan immediately. Be patient for 1 minute—then the steamed mushrooms will have soaked up the mouthwatering flavors.

5 In a bowl, whisk the vinegar with the remaining oil, and season with salt and pepper to taste. Divide the salad greens among 4 serving plates and distribute the mushrooms and pan juices over the top. Scatter the bacon on top, drizzle with the vinaigrette, and toss. Serve now!

Prep time: 30 minutes
Good with: fresh-baked bread
Calories per serving: 330

Caesar Salad
Always a winner

Feeds 4 as a starter:

1 large head romaine lettuce

4 ounces smoked bacon (optional)

2 thin slices white sandwich bread

3 tablespoons vegetable oil

2 cloves garlic

2 eggs (very fresh!)

3-4 tablespoons fresh lemon juice

1/3 cup olive oil

2-3 teaspoons Worcestershire sauce

Salt, freshly ground pepper

2 anchovy fillets (optional)

1 small chunk Parmesan cheese (about 2 ounces)

1 Cut the coarse ribs from the lettuce, wash well, drain, and dry well.

2 Cut the bacon into strips (if using), and sauté in a skillet over medium heat until crisp. Cut the bread into cubes. Remove the bacon from the skillet, pour in the oil, and sauté the bread cubes over medium heat until they become crispy croutons. Peel the garlic and mince it. At the last minute, throw it in with the bread (take care that the garlic doesn't burn).

3 With a pushpin, carefully prick a hole in the eggs and place them in boiling water for 1 minute (max!). Then, dunk them into cold water, crack them open, and pour the still liquidy contents into a medium bowl. Whisk the eggs with the lemon juice, olive oil, and Worcestershire sauce, and season to taste with salt and pepper.

4 Cut the lettuce leaves diagonally into 3/4-inch strips, add them to the bowl, and toss with the dressing. Rinse the anchovy fillets (if using), pat dry, chop, and scatter on top of the salad with the bacon and croutons. Coarsely grate the Parmesan over the top.

Prep time: 30 minutes
Good with: grilled chicken, steak, salmon, or shrimp
Calories per serving: 450

Arugula Salad
Quick to fix and a little bit elegant

Formerly a well-kept Italian secret, but now arugula's in the produce bin at markets here, too. Arugula's great if you've got company, but it's also THE solution for salad-loving singles—one bunch is just right, even for tiny appetites.

Feeds 4 as a starter:

3-4 bunches arugula (at least 10 ounces)

2 tablespoons balsamic vinegar

Salt, freshly ground pepper

1/4 cup good olive oil

10 sun-dried tomatoes marinated in oil

2 thin slices white sandwich bread

1 clove garlic

1-2 tablespoons capers (drained)

1 Cut off any coarse arugula stems, rinse the leaves quickly, and let them drain in a colander. In a small bowl, whisk together the balsamic vinegar, a little salt and pepper, and the olive oil.

2 Remove the tomatoes from their oil and cut into strips. Cube the bread. Heat 1-2 tablespoons of the tomato oil in a skillet and sauté the bread cubes in it over medium heat until brown. Peel the garlic and squeeze it through a garlic press into the skillet; toss with the croutons.

3 Place the arugula in a salad bowl and pour the dressing over the top. Toss well, then scatter the tomato strips, capers, and bread cubes on top. Buon appetito!

Prep time: 25 minutes
Good with: light dry white wine, crusty French bread, or olive bread
Calories per serving: 150

Variations:

With Cheese and Nuts
Instead of tomatoes and croutons, scatter 2 tablespoons pine nuts (toasted quickly in a hot, dry skillet) and 2 tablespoons coarsely grated Parmesan cheese on top of the arugula. Then add the dressing.

With Mushrooms, Prosciutto, and Mozzarella
Omit the tomatoes and croutons. Clean 4 ounces small white mushrooms (wipe off the caps and chop off their little feet) then finely slice and drizzle with 1 tablespoon lemon juice. Cut 4-6 thin slices of prosciutto into fine strips and dice one small ball of fresh mozzarella. Mix with the arugula, season with salt and coarsely ground pepper to taste, and drizzle with the dressing.

With Avocado and Shrimp
Forget about the tomatoes and croutons. Cut one ripe—but not squishy—avocado in half lengthwise. To remove the pit, grasp the two avocado halves and turn them in opposite directions. Peel the avocado, cut it diagonally into thin slices, and drizzle with 1-2 tablespoons lemon juice. Rinse 4 ounces small peeled shrimp and drain well. Wash and halve 4 ounces cherry tomatoes. Throw the avocado, shrimp, and cherry tomatoes in with the arugula and drizzle everything with the dressing.

Vinaigrette
A basic essential

An absolute classic—in addition to dressing salads, vinaigrettes are excellent as marinades for meat and fish, as dips for steamed artichokes, and as basting sauces for broiled or BBQ'd foods. Anyone can custom-create their own "World's Best Vinaigrette" by varying the type of vinegar, oil, and mustard used.

Makes enough for 4:

1 teaspoon Dijon-style mustard

2-3 tablespoons wine vinegar (white or red)

Salt, freshly ground pepper

6 tablespoons oil (sunflower oil, olive oil, part nut oil)

1 In a bowl, whisk together the mustard, vinegar, and salt and pepper to taste. While whisking, dribble in the oil until you have a slightly creamy mixture. Taste again, adjust the seasonings—and that's all there is to it!

Prep time: 2 minutes
Good with: nearly everything that can be called salad
Calories per serving: 110

Variations:

Tomato Vinaigrette
Place 1 tomato briefly in boiling water, dunk it in cold water, and peel off the skin using a paring knife. Chop the tomato into tiny cubes and mix them with the vinaigrette. Tastes great over sliced roast beef, warm lentils, or fresh mozzarella cheese.

Herb Vinaigrette
Wash some fresh herbs of your choice, chop them very finely, and mix them into the vinaigrette to taste just before serving. Hint: use Italian parsley for artichokes, chives for asparagus, and dill for cucumbers or steamed fish fillets.

Yogurt-Herb Dressing
Good tasting and good for you!

Makes enough for 4:

4 ounces plain yogurt (half of an 8-ounce carton)

2 tablespoons fresh lemon juice (or white wine vinegar)

1 tablespoon vegetable oil

Salt, freshly ground pepper

1/2-1 bunch fresh herbs (such as chives, dill, basil)

1 In a bowl, blend the yogurt with the lemon juice (or vinegar) and the oil and stir until smooth. Taste and season with salt and pepper.

2 Wash the herbs, shake dry, chop finely, and stir into the dressing. Taste again and season if necessary.

Prep time: 8 minutes
Good with: green salad, tomato salad, cucumber salad, pasta salad, broiled or BBQ'd vegetables
Calories per serving: 45

Cheese Dressing
Strong or delicate

Makes enough for 4:

2 ounces Roquefort cheese, without the rind

1/4 cup heavy cream

1-2 tablespoons white wine vinegar

Freshly ground pepper

2 tablespoons vegetable oil

or:

2 ounces cream cheese (softened)

1/4 cup plain yogurt

1-2 tablespoons fresh lemon juice

Salt, freshly ground pepper

1 tablespoon vegetable oil

1 If you feel like something potent, choose version #1: crush the Roquefort with a fork in a bowl and stir with the cream until it's smooth. Add the vinegar, and season lightly with pepper. Lastly, blend in the oil.

2 If you feel mellow, choose version #2: stir the cream cheese with the yogurt and lemon juice in a bowl until it's smooth, and add a little salt and pepper. Blend in the oil.

Prep time: (either recipe) 5-10 minutes
Good with: (#1) hardy greens (#2) grated carrots, bean sprouts, radishes, watercress
Calories per serving: (# 1) 510 (# 2) 260

Lemon Vinaigrette
A Mediterranean basic

Makes enough for 4:

1/2 lemon

1-2 tablespoons Dijon-style mustard

Salt, freshly ground pepper

1 clove garlic

4-5 tablespoons olive oil

1 tablespoon water

1 Wash the lemon under hot water, grate the zest, and squeeze the juice. In a bowl, blend together the grated zest, lemon juice, and mustard, and season lightly with salt and pepper.

2 Peel the garlic, push it through a press, and add it to the bowl. While whisking, add the olive oil one spoonful at a time, and then whisk in the water.

Prep time: 10 minutes
Good with: grilled eggplant, zucchini, arugula, white beans, grilled fish or chicken
Calories per serving: 95

Egg Dressing
Almost a salad in its own right

Makes enough for 4:

2 hard-boiled eggs

3 tablespoons white wine vinegar

1 tablespoon mustard

1 tablespoon sour cream

Salt, freshly ground pepper

5 tablespoons vegetable or olive oil

A few fresh basil leaves

1 Peel and rinse the eggs and chop them into tiny cubes.

2 In a bowl, whisk the vinegar with the mustard, sour cream, and salt and pepper to taste. While whisking, add the oil a spoonful at a time; then stir in the chopped egg. Rinse the basil leaves, shake dry, cut into fine strips, and stir into the dressing.

Prep time: 10 minutes
Good with: warm asparagus, sliced fresh mushrooms, watercress. It also makes a nice sauce for cold roast beef and ham.
Calories per serving: 135

German Potato Salad

The world's best potato salad? You be the judge.

Feeds 4 as a side dish:

2¼ pounds boiling potatoes

Salt

1 cup chicken or meat stock

1/4 cup white wine vinegar (or more to taste)

1 teaspoon sharp mustard

Freshly ground pepper

1 onion

1 bunch fresh chives

3-4 tablespoons vegetable oil

1 Wash the potatoes, put them in a pot, just barely cover with water, and bring to a boil. Add 1 teaspoon salt, cover the pot, and simmer over medium heat for 15-20 minutes, until they're tender. Pour off the water, let the potatoes cool for a spell, but peel them while they're still quite hot.

2 Meanwhile, heat up the stock in a saucepan and stir in the vinegar, mustard, and salt and pepper to taste. Peel the onion and mince it. Wash, shake dry, and chop the fresh chives.

3 Slice the warm potatoes—don't worry if they crumble—and put them in a big bowl. Immediately pour over the warm stock mixture, toss well, taste, and season. Let stand briefly. Then, stir in the oil, onion, and chives. You may need a tad more salt, pepper, and/or vinegar.

Prep time: 45 minutes
Good with: sausages, fried chicken, hamburgers, and other picnic stuff
Calories per serving: 260

Pasta Salad
A party favorite

Feeds 6-8:

10 ounces short pasta shapes

Salt

8 ounces cooked ham (or smoked turkey)

6 ounces semi-aged Gouda cheese

1 bunch radishes

1/2 cucumber

1 bunch fresh chives

1 bunch fresh dill

2-3 tablespoons mayonnaise

2-3 tablespoons plain yogurt

2-3 tablespoons white wine vinegar

Freshly ground pepper

2-3 tablespoons vegetable oil

1 Throw the pasta into a pot of boiling salted water and cook at a rolling boil till it's done (check the package for the cooking time, but also taste it occasionally to ensure that the pasta doesn't overcook). Pour the pasta into a colander, shake off the water, and drain well.

2 Meanwhile, cut the ham (or turkey) into strips and coarsely grate the cheese. Cut all the green parts off of the radishes, wash them well, and slice them thinly. Peel the cucumber and cut into small cubes. Wash and chop the herbs.

3 In a bowl, whisk the mayonnaise (of course homemade mayo would be best— see page 92) with the yogurt and vinegar. Season to taste with salt and pepper. Lastly, blend in the oil.

4 In a bowl, mix the pasta with the ham (or turkey), cheese, radishes, cucumber, and herbs. Pour on the dressing, toss well, and let it stand for a few minutes. Taste the salad one more time to see if it needs anything— salt, pepper, vinegar—before the guests hit the buffet.

Prep time: 30 minutes
Good with: anything on the picnic table
Calories per serving (8): 310

Tuscan-Style Bread Salad
Demonstrates the art of using leftovers

Feeds 4-6 as a starter:

6 ounces stale country-style white bread

1 pound ripe tomatoes

1 small red bell pepper

1 small green bell pepper

1 bunch green onions

1/2-1 bunch fresh Italian parsley

1 bunch fresh basil

2 cloves garlic

2-3 tablespoons red wine vinegar

Salt, freshly ground pepper

5 tablespoons good olive oil

1 tablespoon capers (drained)

1 Cut the bread into cubes. Wash and cube the tomatoes, discarding the stems. Wash the peppers, remove the stems, ribs, and seeds, and chop into little cubes. Cut the white and bright green parts of the green onions into fine slices. Mix everything together in a bowl.

2 Wash the herbs, shake dry, and chop finely. Peel and mince the garlic. In a small bowl, mix the vinegar with salt and pepper to taste, and whisk in the oil. Add the capers and toss with the salad ingredients. Set in a cool place until ready to serve.

Prep time: 30 minutes + 1 hour sitting time
Good with: little glasses of red wine
Calories per serving (6): 150

Middle Eastern Wheat Salad
Fresh and easy

Feeds 4:

8 ounces bulgur wheat

1 large bunch green onions

1 pound ripe tomatoes

5-6 tablespoons fresh lemon juice

About 1/2 teaspoon chili powder

1 generous pinch ground star anise

Salt, freshly ground pepper

6 tablespoons good olive oil

Handful of fresh mint leaves

1/2 bunch fresh Italian parsley

1 Pour the bulgur into a bowl, cover well with cold water, and let soak for 1 hour, until the grains have softened, but are still slightly firm to the bite.

2 Wash the green onions, discard any old leaves, cut off the root ends, and chop finely. Wash the tomatoes, remove and discard the stems, and cut into small cubes.

3 Pour the bulgur into a fine mesh sieve, stir vigorously with a spoon, and press to remove as much water as possible. Place the bulgur in a bowl, and mix with the green onions and tomatoes.

4 In a small bowl, whisk the lemon juice with the chili powder, star anise, and salt and pepper to taste. Stir in the olive oil. Toss the dressing with the salad.

5 Wash the mint and parsley, shake dry, coarsely chop or tear the leaves, and mix into the salad. This salad tastes best if it sits for a while before serving.

Prep time: 20 minutes + 1 hour soaking time
Good with grilled lamb, beef, chicken, shrimp, or duck
Calories per serving: 330

Cucumber Salad
A crisp, cool classic

Feeds 4 as a side dish:

1 large cucumber

1 onion

3-4 tablespoons plain yogurt

2-3 tablespoons white wine vinegar

Salt, freshly ground pepper

3 tablespoons vegetable oil

1/2 bunch fresh dill

1 Lightly peel the cucumber, and cut off the stem end. Cut the cucumber into slices or chunks. Peel the onion, cut it in half, and slice thinly.

2 In a salad bowl, blend the yogurt with the vinegar, and a touch of salt and pepper, then whisk in the oil. Wash the dill, shake dry, chop finely, and stir into the dressing. Mix in the cucumber and onion, and let stand for a while before serving to blend the flavors.

Prep time: 10 minutes
Good with: sautéed chicken or turkey tenders, roast pork, fish dishes, other salads
Calories per serving: 95

New Coleslaw
Good and healthy

Feeds 6 as a side dish:

1 head green cabbage (about 2 pounds)

Salt

2 red bell peppers

1 bunch fresh Italian parsley

Freshly ground pepper

5-6 tablespoons white wine vinegar

5-6 tablespoons vegetable oil

1 Discard any wilted cabbage leaves. Quarter the cabbage, and cut away the core. With a knife, shred the cabbage, place the cabbage in a salad bowl, sprinkle with salt, and toss well.

2 Wash the peppers, remove the stems, ribs, and seeds, and cut into thin strips. Wash the parsley, shake dry, and finely chop. Mix both ingredients with the cabbage.

3 In a small bowl, stir a little bit of ground pepper into the vinegar, and whisk in the oil. Pour over the salad, toss well, and let stand for a while to blend the flavors.

Prep time: 30 minutes
Good with: Meat or poultry
Calories per serving: 115

Fresh Green Bean Salad
Just like Grandma's

Feeds 4 as an appetizer or side dish:

1 1/2 pounds fresh thin green beans

Salt

A few fresh thyme leaves

2 onions

2 ounces smoked bacon

3-4 tablespoons white wine vinegar

Freshly ground pepper

2-3 tablespoons vegetable oil

1 Wash the beans, shake dry, and cut off just the ends. Pull off any strings.

2 In a large saucepan, bring 2 quarts of water to boil, add some salt, and throw in the thyme. Add the beans and simmer for 6-8 minutes, until they're tender at first, but still slightly crisp at the center. Drain the beans and rinse under cold water. Cut the larger beans in half. Peel and mince the onions and mix with the drained beans in a bowl.

3 Cut the bacon into little cubes and brown in a skillet until crisp. Swirl the vinegar into the pan. Season with salt and pepper to

taste, and mix in the oil. Pour the bacon dressing over the green bean mixture, and toss well.

Prep time: 30 minutes
Good with: pan-fried potatoes, roasted meats and poultry
Calories per serving; 190

Cold Beef Salad
Make a party dish from your leftovers

Feeds 4 as a snack:

About 1 pound leftover cooked beef

2 small red onions

2 small cornichons (tiny, tart French pickles)

1 tablespoon capers (drained)

2-3 tablespoons white wine vinegar

2 tablespoons vegetable oil

2 tablespoons extra virgin olive oil

Salt, freshly ground pepper

1 bunch fresh chives

1 Cut the cold beef into strips. Peel the onions and cut them into thin rings. Mince the cornichons. Throw the ingredients into a bowl with the capers.

2 Whisk the vinegar with both oils, and season with salt and pepper. Pour the dressing over the salad and let stand for a few minutes. Wash the chives, shake dry, chop into tiny bits, and scatter over the salad.

Prep time: 20 minutes
Good with: crusty French bread
Calories per serving: 310

Salad Variations:

Nonfat Cucumber Salad
Bring 10 tablespoons cider vinegar to a boil with 1 tablespoon sugar. Let cool. Peel a cucumber, cut it lengthwise, and remove the seeds. Thinly slice the cucumber halves on the diagonal. Peel 2 red onions and cut them into thin rings. Add 1/2-3/4 teaspoon red chile flakes to the vinegar mixture, and pour over the salad. Toss well and let stand for a while before serving.

Thai Beef Salad
Mix the leftover beef strips with lots of finely chopped green onion. Make the dressing from 1/4 cup fresh lime juice, 2 tablespoons vegetable oil, 1/2-3/4 teaspoon red chile flakes, 2-3 chopped garlic cloves, and a pinch of sugar. Scatter lots of fresh cilantro leaves over the salad.

Marinated Shrimp
Salad from the sea

Feeds 4:

1 pound small cooked, peeled shrimp

1 small sweet onion

1/4 cup capers (drained)

1/4 cup fresh lemon juice (or more to taste)

1/4 cup extra virgin olive oil

Salt, freshly ground pepper

Tabasco sauce

1/2 bunch fresh dill

1 Rinse the shrimp in a colander and drain well. Peel the onion, cut it in half lengthwise, then cut it lengthwise into thin slices.

2 Place the shrimp in a bowl with the onion, capers, lemon juice, and olive oil and mix well. Season with salt, pepper, and Tabasco sauce to taste. Refrigerate the salad, covered, for 1-24 hours, to blend the flavors.

3 Wash the dill, shake dry, and chop. Mix in into the salad right before serving.

Prep time: 20 minutes, plus marinating time
Good with: bread, boiled new potatoes
Calories per serving: 245

Chinese "Firepot" Fondue
Combine party games and eating into one activity

For this take on fondue, all the ingredients get cooked in freshly prepared chicken stock, instead of a bath of boiling oil. If you're short on time, buy some ready-made chicken stock and dilute it with water—one part stock to two parts water.

Feeds 5 guests + 1 host:

1 ounce dried shiitake mushrooms (look for these in an Asian market)

2 ounces glass or cellophane noodles (ditto)

10 ounces boneless chicken breasts

10 ounces boneless beef sirloin

10 ounces fish fillets (such as salmon, tuna, or halibut)

6-12 large shrimp (1-2 per guest)

2 bunches green onions

10 ounces carrots

1 small head Chinese cabbage (or other fresh vegetables such as spinach, leeks, turnips)

Marinade ingredients (optional):

For the chicken, 2 tablespoons fresh lemon juice, 2 tablespoons sesame oil, and 1 tablespoon chopped fresh ginger. For the beef, 2-3 chopped garlic cloves, some chili powder, freshly ground pepper, and 2-3 tablespoons of peanut oil. For the fish and shrimp, 2 tablespoons each of soy sauce, sesame oil, and lemon juice.

About 3 quarts chicken stock (see Basic Tip)

Condiments, Sauces, Accompaniments:

Ready-made Asian-style sauces, such as soy sauce, plum sauce, hoisin sauce, *sambal oelek*...Fresh chile peppers, hot steamed rice

1 Soften the mushrooms in boiling water for about 30 minutes, then remove the hard stems. Soak the noodles briefly in hot water until softened and drain in a colander. Using kitchen scissors, cut the noodles into small pieces. Cut the chicken, beef, and fish into thin strips and put each into a separate bowl. Peel and rinse the shrimp and put it in another bowl. Wash and trim all of the vegetables, and cut into matchstick strips.

2 If desired, mix together the marinades for the fish and meat.

3 On the other hand, you don't have to use any marinades at all—especially if there are some great dips on the side.

4 Hold on—we're not done yet...bring the stock to a boil in a saucepan. Put all the cut-up ingredients and the sauces into little bowls and set them on the table around the fondue pot or Mongolian hot pot stand. Have some soy sauce handy, too. Wash the fresh chile peppers and cut them into rings—some guests like it really hot! When the stock boils, transfer it to the fondue pot or hot pot and light the heat source.

5 Provide each guest with a small-handled strainer—using fondue forks definitely shows your age! (Comb an Asian market or the Chinatown-section of your city for the strainers—they should be cheap.) Have your guests put something that looks good into their strainer, dip it in the hot stock, and cook it for 1-2 minutes. Then, everyone can dip their food into the condiment of choice and enjoy it. For the grand finale: ladle a taste of the remaining hot stock into little bowls for sipping—it should be chock-full of flavor from all the delicious encounters in the fondue pot.

Prep time: stock–2$\frac{1}{2}$ hours (but it pretty much makes itself), other prep jobs 1 hour
Good with: Chinese beer
Calories per serving: 340

Basic Tip

Homemade Chicken Stock
In a big pot, bring 4 quarts of water to a boil. Throw in 2 peeled and halved onions, 3 chopped carrots, 2 stalks celery, 2 bay leaves, a handful of parsley stems, 1 tablespoon salt, and a few peppercorns. Toss in one 3-pound chicken (but you don't want to make a big splash), reduce the heat to low, and simmer covered for 1$\frac{1}{2}$ hours. Occasionally skim off the foam that rises to the surface. Remove the chicken from the pot (it tastes good cold, chopped-up and tossed with Lemon Vinaigrette—see p 73). Pour the stock through a fine sieve. Skim the fat off the surface of the stock with a big spoon, or blot with a paper towel. Season to taste with salt, pepper, and lemon juice.
Makes about 2 quarts

Noodle Soup
Works miracles when you've got the blues

Feeds 4:

1 pound beef bones

Salt

1¼ pounds beef stew meat

3 carrots

2 stalks celery

2 onions

Handful of parsley stems

A few whole peppercorns

1 bunch green onions

Freshly ground pepper

6 ounces linguine, or other noodles of your choice

1 Rinse the bones and put them in a large pot with 2 quarts cold water. Cover the pot and bring to boil. Season with salt, add the beef, and simmer for about 1 hour over very low heat. Skim off the scum that rises to the surface from time to time.

2 Peel the carrots, wash the celery, and coarsely chop both. Peel and quarter the onions. Add the vegetables, parsley stems, and peppercorns to the pot and continue to simmer gently for another hour.

3 Wash the green onions and chop off any wilted parts and the root ends. Cut the onions into thin slices.

4 Fish the meat out of the soup and chop it into small pieces. Strain the soup, and remove the fat from the surface with a skimmer or paper towel. Bring the broth to a boil once more and season generously.

5 Throw the noodles into the boiling broth and cook until just tender (see instructions on package). Put the chopped meat and green onions in the pot and heat through.

Prep time: a good 2 hours, though you'll only be busy for about 30 minutes
Good with: bread or rolls
Calories per serving: 350

Speedy Minestrone
Grab that spoon and you're ready to go…

Feeds 4-6:

1½ quarts vegetable stock

1 pound boiling potatoes

1 baby leek

2 medium carrots

2 small zucchini

2 stalks celery

2 ripe tomatoes

1 small can beans (8 ounces), drained–try white, kidney, or garbanzo

Salt, freshly ground pepper

2 teaspoons prepared pesto

2 ounces Parmesan or Romano cheese, freshly grated

1 Pour the stock into a large pot, cover, and bring to a boil. Wash the potatoes, peel, and cut them into cubes. Slide off the lid of the pot and throw in the potatoes. Slit the leek lengthwise down the center, wash it well (be sure to get all of the sand that's stuck between the layers), cut it into strips, and toss them into the pot. Peel the carrots, cut them into slices, and toss them into the pot. Wash the zucchini and celery stalks, discard any wilted parts, cut into strips or slices, and toss them into the pot.

2 Plunge the tomatoes into boiling water for a few seconds and rinse in cold water. With a paring knife, remove the peels. Cube the tomato meat and throw it in the pot with the drained beans. Cover the pot and continue to simmer the soup for 15-20 more minutes over low heat. Add salt and pepper to taste. Stir in the pesto and grated cheese.

Prep time: 45 minutes
Good with: fresh garlic bread
Calories per serving (6): 280

Potato Soup
Super-cheap and super-tasty

If you want to spend a bit more, soak some dried porcini mushrooms in boiling water to soften, then chop, and add to the soup at the last minute. Delish!

Feeds 4:

1½ pounds baking potatoes

2 onions

1 leek

2 carrots

4 ounces smoked bacon

1 tablespoon butter (or vegetable oil)

1½ quarts chicken or meat stock

1 bay leaf

1/2 teaspoon dried marjoram

Salt, freshly ground pepper

Freshly ground nutmeg

1 Peel the potatoes and cut them into small cubes. Peel and mince the onions. Slit the leek lengthwise, wash well—don't forget between the layers—and cut into very thin rings. Peel and cube the carrots. Cube the bacon, too.

2 Heat the butter (or oil) in a stockpot over medium heat. Throw in the bacon and onions and sauté until the onions are translucent. Stir in the leek and carrots and sauté briskly. Add the stock, bay leaf, and dried marjoram, and season with a little salt and pepper. Simmer covered for 30 minutes.

3 Puree or mash the vegetables a little in the pot—use a hand blender or potato masher. Add salt, pepper, and nutmeg to taste.

Prep time: 1 hour
Good with: sausages, crusty bread
Calories per serving: 340

Tomato Soups
Takes 12 minutes or 12 hours

Feeds 4 impatient people:

1 onion

2 tablespoons vegetable oil

1 large can peeled tomatoes (28 ounces)

2 cups chicken stock

4 ounces Roquefort cheese (crumbled)

Salt, freshly ground pepper

1/2 teaspoon *sambal oelek* or other hot chile paste

1 Peel the onion and finely chop. In a saucepan, heat the oil over medium heat and sauté the onion in it until it's translucent. Pour in the tomatoes with their juice, crush them in the pot, and add the stock. Let the ingredients get very hot for about 5 minutes. Stir in the cheese. Season to taste with salt, pepper, and *sambal oelek*.

Feeds 4 patient people:

2 onions

2 cloves garlic

About 2 pounds very ripe tomatoes

1 tablespoon chopped fresh basil

Salt, freshly ground pepper

1/4 cup olive oil

2 teaspoons tomato paste

3 cups chicken stock

1 pinch sugar

2-3 tablespoons gin

1/4 cup heavy cream

1 Peel and chop the onions and garlic. Wash the tomatoes, remove the stems, and cube. In a bowl, mix the tomatoes, onions, garlic, basil, and a little salt and pepper. Cover and let stand in a cool place for 12 hours.

2 Heat the oil in a skillet over medium heat. Stir in the tomato mixture and tomato paste, then pour in the stock. Simmer the soup gently for 5 minutes, and season to taste with salt and pepper. Stir in the sugar and gin. Just before serving, stir the cream into the soup.

Prep time: 12 minutes or 12 hours
Good with (both recipes): garlic croutons
Calories per serving: (impatient soup): 180, (patient soup): 185

Cream of Pumpkin Soup
Fast and fabulous

Feeds 4:

$2\frac{1}{2}$ pounds pumpkin (bright orange sweet pumpkin tastes best)

1 onion

2 tablespoons butter

1 quart vegetable stock

Salt, freshly ground pepper

Fresh lemon juice (or balsamic vinegar)

1 With a sturdy vegetable peeler, peel the pumpkin. Cut it in half and remove the seeds and strings. Chop the pumpkin meat into small pieces.

2 Peel and finely chop the onion. In a large saucepan, melt the butter over medium heat. Add the onion and sauté until translucent; stir in the pumpkin meat. Pour in the stock, cover the pan, and bring to a boil. Reduce the heat slightly and simmer the soup for 10-15 minutes, until the pumpkin is soft.

3 Using a hand blender, puree the pumpkin in the pan and season well to taste with salt, pepper, and lemon juice (or vinegar).

Prep time: 30 minutes
Good with: ginger, curry powder, or soy sauce to taste; roasted pumpkin seeds or almonds scattered on top
Calories per serving: 130

Gazpacho
Tastes like the sun in Spain

Feeds 4:

$1\frac{1}{2}$ pounds very ripe tomatoes

1 cucumber

1 green bell pepper

2 onions

3 cloves garlic

3 thin slices white sandwich bread

1-2 tablespoons red wine vinegar

1/2 cup water

3 tablespoons olive oil

Salt, freshly ground pepper

1 tablespoon butter

1 Set aside 2-3 of the tomatoes. Plunge the rest in boiling water for one minute, then rinse well in cold water. With a paring knife, remove the peels. Cut the peeled tomatoes into smaller pieces, discarding the stems.

2 Wash and halve the cucumber, and set one half aside. Peel the other half and cut it into small pieces. Halve and wash the bell pepper, set one half aside, and cut the other into squares.

3 Peel and mince 1 of the onions. Peel the garlic. Puree both together with the chopped vegetables. Drizzle 2 slices of the bread with vinegar and water. Add the soaked bread to the vegetable mixture with the oil and puree all ingredients until smooth. Season with salt and pepper to taste. Cover and refrigerate for 2-3 hours.

4 Now, finely dice all of the remaining vegetables. Cube the remaining slice of the bread and sauté it in the butter until golden brown and crispy. Scatter the diced vegetables and bread cubes in the cold soup just before serving.

Prep time: 45 minutes doing things, 2-3 hours to cool down
Calories per serving: 200

Fish Soup
Revives weary spirits

The secret to making good soup is to start with good stock. Homemade stock is always preferred.

Stock—makes 1 quart:

About 2 pounds fish trimmings (heads and

bones of lean white fish—avoid salmon)

1 onion

2 cloves garlic

1 leek

1-2 carrots

2 stalks celery

1 small bulb fennel

5 cups water

2 cups dry white wine

2 bay leaves

1 teaspoon white peppercorns

Salt

1 Rinse the fish trimmings well and put them in a pot. Peel and coarsely chop the onion and garlic. Slit the leek lengthwise, rinse well (remember to get between the layers), and cut into small pieces. Peel the carrots and chop into chunks. Wash and trim the celery and fennel and chop both into medium chunks.

2 Put all of the vegetables in the pot with the fish trimmings, and add the water, wine, bay leaves, and peppercorns. Cover and bring to a boil, then remove the lid and simmer over medium heat for 20-30 minutes; regularly skim off the foam that rises to the top. Pour the contents of the pot through a fine sieve into a clean pot, and continue to simmer until about 1 quart of stock remains. Season with salt to taste.

Soup—feeds 4:

1 onion

2 cloves garlic

2 carrots

1 small leek

2 stalks celery

2-3 tablespoons olive oil

1 quart fish stock (see above)

Salt, freshly ground pepper

1-2 tablespoons crème fraîche

18 ounces fish fillets (whatever's the catch

of the day—now you can go for the salmon)

1 handful fresh chervil (or arugula)

1-2 tablespoons fresh lemon juice

1 Peel and finely chop the onion and garlic. Wash and trim the remaining vegetables, and cut into matchstick strips. Throw them all into a wide saucepan and sauté over medium heat in the olive oil, until the onion is translucent. Pour in the fish stock, add a little salt and pepper, cover, and boil for 3-4 minutes. Reduce the heat and stir in the crème fraîche.

2 Cut the fish into 1-inch pieces. Place the fish pieces in the stock mixture, and let stand for 3-5 minutes over low heat. Wash, shake dry, and finely chop the chervil (or arugula). Carefully stir in the lemon juice so that the fish doesn't fall apart before serving.

Prep time: 1-1½ hours for the stock, 40 minutes for the soup
Good with: green salad, French bread
Calories per serving: 310

Sauce & Dip

Life without sauce would be only half as much fun...

Believe you can live without sauce?

Just think—roast beef or mashed potatoes with no gravy would be only half as much fun. Chicken skewers would be bland without the spicy peanut sauce on the side. Vegetables would be plain-old vegetables without the aïoli or other dipping sauce.

You might be under the impression that sauces take a lot of time to prepare and yield too little results. True, some cooks are known for going into the kitchen with a whole bucketful of ingredients, then, four hours later, coming back out again with a tiny cup of sauce. Though some types of sauces take a lot of time and effort to prepare, there are others that are ready in a snap.

Think of it this way. Everyone has a different taste in music, sometimes even changing depending on his or her mood. Sauce makes food better the same way music makes life better. Sometimes a quick little ditty does the trick, and sometimes we crave an elaborate operatic composition. We can live without music (and sauce), but why?

A true culinary artist can coax the best out of his or her ingredients to make a really good sauce—whether super-simple or highly complex. The choice is yours—from soy sauce, to pesto, to Provençal vegetable ragout.

Our Favorite Ingredient
The Egg
French: oeuf; Italian: uovo;
Spanish: huevo

Eggs have:
- 70 calories per large egg
- 6 grams of pure protein
- hardly any carbohydrates
- a decent dose of calcium, phosphorus, iron, and vitamins A, E, and B$_2$

Eggs can:
- take in air when beaten, which makes sauces fluffy
- thicken when heated and give body to hollandaise and other "emulsion" sauces
- be the tie that binds, such as between the fat and liquid components of mayonnaise

Eggs need:
- a happy Mama. Well, a free-range chicken or one that can go outdoors. The others live in cages and live a less-than-enjoyable life
- to be freshly laid. Fresh eggs—bought from the farm–should be no more than 7 days old. Be sure to check the expiration date on the ones you get from the supermarket
- to be stored in the refrigerator, and to be brought to room temperature, if possible, before using
- to be cooked properly: boil for 3-4 minutes for soft yolks, 5-6 minutes for medium yolks, 10 minutes for hard yolks

Eggs love:
- something acidic–wine, vinegar, or lemon juice–in a sauce
- herbs, such as dill, tarragon, Italian parsley, or chervil
- solid companions, like bacon, cheese, or onions
- salt–but added at the last minute, otherwise scrambled eggs go sloppy and fried eggs get spotty

Enrich sauces with dairy products

Cream
Milk fat (about 30% in heavy cream) makes sauces taste both smoother and richer. Whipping cream into stiff peaks before mixing makes a sauce light and fluffy in texture. But too much cream can weigh you down after a while. A better option is to make a good basic sauce, then pep it up at the last minute with a touch of fresh cream. Or, omit the cream altogether when using super-fresh, bold-flavored sauce ingredients.

Crème fraîche
Crème fraîche is a smooth, tangy substance similar to sour cream, only better! The tang comes from beneficial bacteria—the stuff that's in buttermilk and sour cream. You can find crème fraîche in tubs in a specialty or gourmet foods store, or you can make it yourself: Put 1 cup heavy cream in a glass jar and stir in 2 tablespoons of buttermilk. Let it stand, covered, at room temperature overnight, then refrigerate it until you're ready to use it. Crème fraîche can be used both to round out sauces and to bind them. In this case, too, less is definitely more.

Yogurt
Yogurt gives a special flair to long-simmered hot sauces, such as the ones used for stewed or braised meats—think Asian-style dishes like lamb curry. Yogurt also freshens up cold sauces and dips with its sourish flavor, and it makes your creations smooth— yet still low fat—with its 3-4% butterfat content.

Don't forget ...
Mascarpone—the newly chic extra-rich Italian cream cheese—is not only great for tiramisu. A spoonful of it can tone down a piquant Gorgonzola sauce to make it more interesting. Cream cheese and sour cream can also add pizzazz to sauces and dips. And ultra-low-fat buttermilk can give all the tingle of sour cream to a sauce or dip with little of its calories.

The Roux is Back

For ages, creative cooks have tried to think of a better way to make sauces than with the tried-and-true roux (a cooked mixture of fat and flour used to thicken sauces and soups). Cream, butter, eggs, vegetable purees, ground nuts....all are delicious solutions, but the sauces are never quite the same.

Nowadays, when the old is new again, trendsetters are rediscovering roux. Often, using roux at the beginning makes a better sauce than by infusing it with huge amounts of butter at the end.

The secret to roux is heat. Heat makes the flour "sweat" so it gets sticky enough to bind with the fat. Hot fat will ensure that the roux doesn't burn or get too runny. With the right heat, the flour can suck up the fat so that lumps won't form when the sauce's liquid is added.

Basic directions for making a roux-based sauce:

1 In a heavy skillet or saucepan (do not use nonstick), melt 2 tablespoons butter. Stir in 2 tablespoons flour—it will foam at first, but keep stirring and you'll get a light, smooth, solid mass. Cook, stirring, until the mass turns very light brown. If you want a darker sauce, cook the roux until it turns light golden brown. For a very dark, nutty flavored sauce, cook the roux until it's deep golden brown.

2 Now, pour in 2 cups of lukewarm liquid—such as milk (for white sauce) or chicken stock (for gravy)—and whisk continuously. Heat quickly over fairly high heat, whisking to ensure that nothing burns and the sauce stays smooth.

3 Slow down with the whisk and simmer the sauce for 10 minutes to cook away the flour taste. And there you have it: Basic sauce.

In

A good sauce base • a supply of homemade stocks and sauces frozen in ice cube trays • being bold when adding spices • sticking to a few good things • sauces made from pureed vegetables • chutneys • unusual "dippers," such as tiny cooked potatoes, asparagus spears, green beans • bread for sopping up the leftover sauce • *Always in style: licking the plate clean (only among friends)*

Out

Ready-made sauces • using the sauce pot as a waste-disposal unit for bad wine • the same old spices • using a one-size-fits-all sauce every day • adding ingredients willy-nilly • stale garlic in the dip • drowning bad food in good sauce • forgetting the recipe for a quick and tasty sauce • *Never, ever in style: serving spaghetti with red sauce at a formal wedding (even among friends)*

Five 5-Minute Savory Sauces

Fast Pasta Sauce
Sauté some chopped garlic and dried oregano in olive oil, then stir in 2 tablespoons tomato paste. Add a can of crushed tomatoes, some sliced pitted olives, a few capers, and chopped anchovies. Bring to a boil, add bits of canned tuna and chopped fresh Italian parsley, and heat through.

Fast Fish Sauce
Grate a small piece of cucumber, sauté it in a little bit of oil, and add a dash of white wine, and a good spoonful of crème fraîche. Cook till it's thick and creamy. Add chopped fresh dill, mustard, and salt to taste.

Fast Steak Sauce
Sauté some sliced onions in butter with a good pinch of sugar, until browned. Add a dash of balsamic vinegar and a little stock and cook until the liquid becomes syrupy. Add lots of pepper and stir in some fresh basil shreds.

Fast Vegetable Sauce
Toast some curry powder and fennel seeds together in a dry pan, until they smell aromatic. Add a can of diced tomatoes and a tub of plain yogurt, and simmer for 5 minutes. Add salt and sugar to taste. Mix in some steamed vegetable pieces, or braise vegetables right in the sauce.

Fast Dip
Finely chop some fresh mushrooms and stir them with a little lemon juice, chopped fresh chives, pepper, and just enough sour cream to make a thick dip. It's delicious with boiled new potatoes or other vegetables—even crackers or potato chips.

Creamy Green Sauce
One of the simplest!

This old-fashioned, German-style recipe uses several different herbs. Vary the herb types and amounts according to your personal taste.

Makes enough for 4-6:

1 bunch fresh chives

1/2 bunch fresh Italian parsley

1 handful fresh chervil

4 fresh sorrel leaves

5 sprigs fresh tarragon

5 sprigs fresh basil

2 hard-boiled eggs

1 cup crème fraîche

1¹/₂ cups cottage cheese

1/4 cup mayonnaise

1 teaspoon sharp mustard

Worcestershire sauce to taste

Salt, freshly ground pepper

1 Wash all the herbs, shake very dry, and cut away the hard stems. Using a large knife, chop the herbs finely on a large cutting board. Don't use a blender or food processor—it makes the herbs taste bitter.

2 Peel, rinse, and dice the eggs. Mix them with the herbs and rest of the ingredients, seasoning to taste, and let stand for 1 hour before serving.

Prep time: 30 minutes working on it, 1 hour relaxing
Good with: cottage fries, boiled new potatoes, roast beef, grilled fish
Calories per serving (6): 255

Salsa Verde
(Italian green sauce)

Use 2 hard-boiled eggs for this one too, plus a handful of herbs, preferably Italian parsley. Throw in 5-6 anchovy fillets, 2 cloves garlic, 3-4 tablespoons capers, and at least 5 tablespoons of good olive oil. The first thing you do is puree just the egg yolks with the parsley, anchovies, garlic, capers, and oil. Then, add 1-2 tablespoons white wine vinegar, and salt and pepper to taste. Finely chop the egg whites and mix them in. This sauce is really great with sautéed fish, shrimp, and Mediterranean vegetables.

Pesto
Keep a supply in the freezer!

Real pesto purists haul their Italian grandmother's big mortar and pestle out from storage to get pesto's proper texture. In a pinch, a blender works too—the texture might not be ideal, but it will be much faster to make.

Makes enough for 4:

1 large bunch fresh basil

3 tablespoons pine nuts

3 cloves garlic

Salt

1/2 cup olive oil

2 ounces Parmesan or Romano cheese, freshly grated

1 Wash the basil quickly, and make sure it is really dry before using. Pull the basil leaves from their stems.

2 In a dry nonstick skillet, toast the pine nuts very lightly—remove them from the heat as soon as they start to smell good.

3 Peel the garlic and chop it roughly. Mash it to a paste with the basil, pine nuts, and a pinch of salt in a mortar and pestle—or puree the ingredients in a blender. Transfer the paste to a bowl.

4 Then, stir in the olive oil and grated cheese, until you get a smooth creamy sauce. Add salt to taste—and that's it!

Prep time: 20 minutes
Good with: spaghetti or other thin pasta, potatoes, minestrone, vegetable dishes, fish, chicken, and meat. Also good as a spread for sandwiches.
Calories per serving: 240

Basic Tip

Winter Pesto:
Use the same steps as for regular pesto, but use Italian parsley instead of basil, walnuts or almonds instead of pine nuts, shallots instead of garlic, sunflower oil instead of olive oil, and good-quality Swiss cheese instead of Parmesan.

Guacamole
Basic Tex-Mex

Makes enough for 4-6:

2 very ripe avocados (make sure they're soft when you press them)

6-7 tablespoons fresh lemon juice

1 onion

2 cloves garlic

1-2 fresh chile peppers

2 medium-sized ripe tomatoes

2 tablespoons olive oil (optional)

Salt, freshly ground pepper

Pinch of ground coriander

1/2 bunch fresh cilantro

1 Using a knife, cut the avocados lengthwise around the pit. Turn the avocado halves in opposite directions and separate them. Remove the pits, peel the avocado halves, and place them in a bowl. Immediately mix in the lemon juice so that the avocados don't discolor.

2 Peel and mince the onion and garlic. Slit the chile peppers lengthwise, and remove the stems and seeds. Wash the chiles, shake dry, and finely chop.

3 Plunge the tomatoes into boiling water for 1 minute, and rinse in cold water. With a paring knife, remove the skins, and chop the tomatoes into tiny cubes. Mix the onion, garlic, chiles, and tomatoes with the avocado puree, stir in the oil (if using), and add salt, pepper, and coriander powder to taste. Wash the cilantro, shake dry, finely chop, and mix in with the other ingredients.

Prep time: 25 minutes
Good with: tortilla chips, vegetable sticks, steamed fish, and BBQ'd meat
Calories per serving (6): 100

Tzatziki
Garlicky cucumber dip

Makes enough for 4:

2½-3 cups plain yogurt

1 firm cucumber

Salt

3 cloves garlic

1 tablespoon white wine vinegar

1-2 tablespoons olive oil

Chopped fresh mint leaves (optional)

1 Place a coffee filter in a sieve. Spoon in the yogurt, and set it over the sink to drain.

2 Peel the cucumber, grate it coarsely, and put it in a bowl. Mix in 1 teaspoon salt, and let it stand for 10 minutes to draw out some of the liquid. Then, transfer the cucumber to a colander, and with a spoon, press out as much liquid as possible. Mix it with the drained yogurt in a bowl.

3 Peel the garlic, push it through a garlic press, and add it to the other ingredients in the bowl. Stir in the vinegar and oil, and add more salt to taste. Stir in the chopped mint leaves (if using) to taste.

Prep time: 30 minutes
Good with: meat, vegetables, flatbread
Calories per serving: 270

Mango Chutney
Hot and sweet

Makes 2 quarts:

3 ripe mangos (about 2½ pounds)

1 ripe pineapple (2¼-2½ pounds)

1 red bell pepper

2 fresh red chile peppers

2 ounces fresh ginger

2 ounces raisins

2/3 cup sugar

1 tablespoon salt

1 cup cider vinegar

2-3 onions

1-2 cloves garlic

2 lemons

1 teaspoon mustard seeds

1 teaspoon ground allspice

1 With a large knife, carefully cut the fruit away from the large, flat seeds that run lengthwise down the mangos. Peel the fruit and cut it into cubes. With the knife, scrape as much fruit as possible from the seeds. Peel the pineapple and cut it into cubes, avoiding the hard central core.

2 Halve the bell pepper and chile peppers lengthwise. Remove the stems, ribs, and seeds. Wash all the peppers and cut them into small pieces. Peel the ginger and slice it thinly. Coarsely chop the raisins.

3 Put the mangos, pineapple, peppers, ginger, and raisins in a big pot, (don't use aluminum) and mix with the sugar, salt, and vinegar. Cover and let stand overnight, or at least for a few hours.

4 Now, peel and finely chop the onions and garlic, squeeze the juice out of the lemons, and add everything to the pot, including the spices, and mix well.

5 Cover the pot and bring to a boil over medium heat. Then, turn down the heat and gently simmer the mixture, uncovered, for another 30 minutes, until the chutney thickens. Stir frequently and watch carefully to ensure that nothing burns.

6 Let the chutney cool, and use right away. If you're stocking up, pour the chutney while very hot into glass jars, which have been soaked in boiling-hot water for 10-15 minutes (soak the jar lids for 5 minutes). Immediately screw on the lids.

Prep time: 1 hour, plus time to rest overnight
Good with: anything BBQ'd, rice
Calories per quart: 920

Pickled Applesauce
Great for barbecues

Makes enough for 4:

1 tart apple

1 tablespoon fresh lemon juice

1 onion

1-2 cornichons (tiny tart French pickles)

3/4-1 cup sour cream

2-3 tablespoons mayonnaise

2 tablespoons prepared horseradish

Salt, freshly ground pepper

Fresh chives or dill

1 Peel, quarter, and dice the apple and drizzle it with the lemon juice. Peel and finely chop the onion. Cut the pickles into cubes.

2 In a bowl, combine the sour cream with the mayonnaise and horseradish. Season to taste with salt and pepper, and mix in the apple, onion, and pickles. Rinse the herbs, shake dry, finely chop, and stir into the sauce to taste.

Prep time: 10 minutes
Good with: fondue, BBQ'd meats, meatballs
Calories per serving: 150

Peanut Sauce
A new staple

Makes enough for 4:

2-3 tablespoons vegetable oil

2 tablespoons mild curry paste

1 can unsweetened coconut milk (14 ounces)

5 ounces crunchy peanut butter

2 tablespoons sugar

Salt

3 tablespoons rice vinegar (or cider vinegar)

Sambal oelek or other hot chile paste

1 Heat the oil in a small saucepan over medium heat, stir in the curry paste, and sauté lightly until the smell is noticeable. Then, pour in the coconut milk, mix well, and simmer gently for 1-2 minutes.

2 Stir in the peanut butter, sugar, salt to taste, and the vinegar. Simmer for another 5-10 minutes, until the sauce is slightly smooth. Taste and season with *sambal oelek* and salt to taste.

Prep time: 15 minutes
Good with: chicken saté or other Asian-style meat dishes, vegetables, rice, pasta
Calories per serving: 320

Tuna Dip
An easy, mouth-watering blend

Makes enough for 4:

1 can tuna in water (6 ounces)

2 cloves garlic

2 tablespoons capers (drained)

2 tablespoons fresh lemon juice

1 shot dry white wine

2 tablespoons olive oil

2 tablespoons crème fraîche

Salt, freshly ground pepper

1 Drain the tuna. Peel and halve the garlic cloves. With a hand blender or regular blender, puree the tuna and garlic with the capers, lemon juice, wine, and oil.

2 Pour the mixture into a bowl, stir in the crème fraîche, and season with salt and pepper to taste.

Prep time: 10 minutes
Good with: crusty French bread, breadsticks, raw or lightly cooked vegetables, baked or boiled potatoes
Calories per serving: 150

Homemade Mayo
Easy and Impressive

The egg really has to be super-fresh here, because the yolks are mixed in and eaten raw. If you're really concerned about the safety of the eggs, you can use pasteurized frozen egg yolks. If you want to cut back on the oil, add a bit of plain yogurt in at the end—it'll still give you a thick and creamy mayo, but with fewer fat calories.

Makes enough for 4:

1 very fresh, room-temperature egg (you'll only need the yolk for this recipe)

Salt

1 tablespoon Dijon-style mustard

1/2-1 tablespoon fresh lemon juice

About 1/2 cup vegetable oil or olive oil

Freshly ground pepper

1 Separate the egg white from the yolk, and slide the yolk into a bowl (read the Basic Tip below for suggestions on using the egg white). Add a pinch of salt, the mustard, and about 1/2 tablespoon of the lemon juice, and blend really well.

2 Now, mix continuously with a whisk (or electric mixer, if you're so inclined). First, just drizzle in a few drops of the oil and beat well. After the initial oil is incorporated, you can add the oil in a steady trickle, remembering to beat the whole time. Take care that the oil you're adding doesn't form a little puddle on the top of the mixture—it should disappear in the soft, creamy sauce, and bind with the egg yolk.

3 The mixture will gradually turn into a thickish, creamy mayonnaise. When you've added all the oil, stir it just a tad more until you get the consistency you want. Add salt, pepper, and more lemon juice to taste.

Prep time: 15 minutes
Good with: everything—from French fries to artichokes—it's really just a matter of taste
Calories per serving: 170

Basic Tip

Use the leftover egg whites to make Fried Batter with Mascarpone (p 158) or a giant scrambled egg platter (just throw them in with some whole eggs and scramble them all together).

Variations:

Garlic Mayo
Peel and press some garlic, and mix it in with the egg yolk right from the start. How much should you add? It depends on your mood, but 2 small cloves is a good starting point. Goes with: pan-fried fish, vegetable dishes, and fondue.

Lemon Mayo
Cut a lemon in half, squeeze the juice from one half, and stir it in with the egg yolk. Finely grate the zest from the other lemon half, and blend it in with the mayo when it's ready to serve. Goes with: fish, cold roast beef, asparagus, artichokes, shrimp, and cracked crab.

Herbed Mayo
When the mayo's ready, stir in lots of freshly chopped herbs, such as Italian parsley, chives, dill, or basil. This one's also good with a little minced garlic. Goes really well with BBQ'd summer vegetables, baked mushrooms, or sandwiches as a spread.

Remoulade (French-style tartar sauce)
To the finished mayonnaise, add 1-2 cornichons (chopped), 1/2 onion (minced), 1 anchovy fillet (minced), a handful of fresh Italian parsley, chives, or dill (minced) and 1 tablespoon capers (drained); stir everything in well. You might want to spice it up a little with cayenne pepper and hot mustard. Enjoy it with roast beef, pan-fried breaded fish, and everything else already mentioned above.

Provençal Vegetable Ragout
An easy, southern French-style sauce

This sauce is also perfect for marinating a large roast, or as the braising liquid for beef rolls—brown the meat first, then add it to a pot with some sauce before braising.

Makes enough for 4:

10 ounces ripe tomatoes

6 ounces eggplant (the Asian ones are about the right size)

6 ounces zucchini

1 small red or yellow bell pepper

1 medium onion

2-3 cloves garlic

3-4 tablespoons olive oil

1 sprig fresh rosemary

3 tablespoons water

Salt, freshly ground pepper

1/2 cup heavy cream

1 tablespoon balsamic vinegar

5-10 tablespoons vegetable stock (optional)

1 Plunge the tomatoes briefly in boiling water, then rinse under cold water. Peel off the skins using a paring knife. Dice the tomatoes, discarding the stems. Wash the eggplant and zucchini, and remove the stems. First cut the vegetables into slices, then into cubes. Halve the bell pepper, and remove the stems, ribs, and seeds. Wash the peppers and cut them into small squares.

2 Peel and finely chop the onion and garlic. Heat 2 tablespoons of the olive oil over medium heat in a heavy saucepan. Add the onion and garlic and sauté until translucent. Then, throw the rest of the vegetables into the pan. Add the rosemary, the remaining 1-2 tablespoons oil, the water, and salt and pepper to taste. Cover and simmer over low heat for about 40 minutes.

3 Take off the lid, pour in the cream, and stir the contents of the pot really well. Heat the mixture until heated through. Then remove the pot from heat and remove the rosemary. Add salt and pepper to taste, and the balsamic vinegar. If you prefer, you can puree the vegetables to make a smooth, velvety sauce. If you the sauce seems too thick, thin it with a splash or two of stock.

Prep time: 1¼ hours
Good with: roasted lamb, roasted pork, baked fish, or boiled potatoes
Calories per serving: 195

Mojo
Salsa from Spain
red or green

Makes enough for 4:

4 medium cloves garlic

2-3 fresh red or green chile peppers

2 teaspoons sweet paprika (omit if you're making green mojo)

1/2 teaspoon ground cumin

1/2 teaspoon dried oregano (for green mojo: 2 tablespoons chopped fresh Italian parsley, or 1 tablespoon chopped fresh cilantro)

3 tablespoons red or white wine vinegar

3 tablespoons olive oil

Water (optional)

Salt, freshly ground pepper

1 Peel and coarsely chop the garlic. Halve each chile lengthwise, remove the stems and seeds, wash them, and chop coarsely.

2 With a hand blender or regular blender, mix the chiles with the garlic, paprika (if using), cumin, oregano (parsley or cilantro if making green mojo), vinegar, and oil until smooth.

3 If the mojo seems too thick, dilute it with several tablespoons of water. Season with salt and pepper to taste.

Prep time: 15 minutes
Good with: baked potatoes, BBQ'd meats, tacos and burritos, eggs, vegetables, or tortilla chips.
Calories per serving: 75

Variation:
Chunky Tomato Salsa

Plunge 1 pound tomatoes in boiling water for 1 minute, rinse under cold water, and remove the skins with a paring knife. Chop the tomatoes, discarding the stems, and mix with the mojo.

Carrot-Ginger
Sauce
Spicy and fruity

Makes enough for 4:

1 small onion

1 piece fresh ginger (thumb-sized)

1 pound carrots

2 tablespoons vegetable oil

1 teaspoon curry powder

1 cup vegetable stock

1/4 teaspoon ground cumin

Pinch of sugar

Chili powder

Salt, freshly ground pepper

Juice from 1 orange

1 Peel and mince the onion and ginger. Peel the carrots, too, and cut them into slices.

2 Heat the oil in a saucepan over medium heat. Add the onion and ginger and sauté for 1-2 minutes. Stir in the carrots, sprinkle with the curry powder, and sauté, stirring constantly, until the carrots are slightly softened. Then, pour in the stock. Season with the cumin, sugar, just a tad of chili powder, and salt and pepper to taste.

3 Cover the pot and simmer the mixture for 20 minutes. Then, remove the pot from the stove. Using a potato masher, hand blender, or food mill (see photo), crush the carrots into a coarse puree.

4 Pour in the orange juice, and cook the mixture gently, stirring well, until heated through. Add salt and pepper to taste.

Prep time: 35 minutes
Good with: roasted chicken breasts, fish fillets, or a plateful of rice (sprinkle some chopped fresh parsley on top)
Calories per serving: 90

Watermelon
BBQ Sauce
Sounds strange, but
it's unbelievably good

Makes enough for 4:

1 piece well-chilled watermelon (about 18 ounces unpeeled, 10 ounces peeled)

2 onions

4-6 tablespoons ketchup

1 teaspoon honey

Salt, cayenne pepper

1 Peel the watermelon and cut into chunks, removing all of the seeds.

2 Peel and coarsely chop the onions. With a hand blender or regular blender, blend the watermelon and onions to a fine puree with the ketchup and honey. Add salt and cayenne pepper to taste. Serve immediately (or keep in the refrigerator until ready to use).

Prep time: 10 minutes
Good with: anything grilled
Calories per serving: 50

Herbed Pea Sauce
Cool and tasty

Peas in the pod picked straight from the garden are really hard to find these days. If you do come across them, you'll want to serve them up fresh, tossed lightly in butter and sprinkled with fresh herbs. Frozen peas are a good stand-in for this ultra-simple sauce.

Makes enough for 4:

1 small onion

1 tablespoon butter

1 box frozen peas (10 ounces)

1/2 cup dry white wine

1/2 cup heavy cream

Salt, freshly ground pepper

1/2 bunch fresh basil

Fresh lemon juice

1 Peel, halve, and mince the onion. In a tall saucepan, melt the butter over medium heat, throw in the onion, and sauté until the onion is translucent.

2 Open the box of peas, pour them into the pan, and mix with the onion. Pour in the wine, pour in the cream, and season with salt and pepper to taste. Cover the pan and bring the mixture to a boil.

3 Rinse the basil, shake dry well, and remove the leaves. Add a couple of leaves to the pan right away and simmer, covered, for 5 minutes.

4 Remove the pan from the heat, add the remaining basil leaves, and puree the contents of the pot with a hand blender. Add more salt, pepper, and a couple squirts of lemon juice to taste.

Prep time: 15 minutes
Good with: warm hard-boiled eggs, salmon, pork tenderloin
Calories per serving: 190

Mushroom Sauce
A versatile sauce that will become a staple

Makes enough for 4:

1¼ pounds fresh mushrooms (white, brown, chanterelle, and/or porcini)

3 tablespoons fresh lemon juice

1 onion

1/2 bunch fresh Italian parsley

2 tablespoons butter

Salt, freshly ground pepper

3/4 cup heavy cream

1 Don't wash the mushrooms: wipe them clean with a damp cloth and slice off the bottoms of the stems. Slice the mushrooms thinly and drizzle them with 2 tablespoons of the lemon juice—so they don't discolor. Peel and finely chop the onion. Wash the parsley, shake it dry, and finely chop it.

2 In a big skillet, melt the butter over medium heat. Add the onion and sauté until translucent. Then, increase the heat slightly, add the mushrooms to the pan handful by handful, and sauté, stirring constantly. Once all the mushrooms are sautéed, season them with salt and pepper, mix in half of the parsley, and pour in the cream.

3 Simmer the mushrooms gently over medium-low heat for 10 minutes. The last step: add the remaining tablespoon of lemon juice, season with salt and pepper to taste, and sprinkle with the rest of the fresh parsley.

Prep time: 30 minutes
Good with: pasta, potatoes, pancakes (see p 52), fried chicken, steak
Calories per serving: 210

Curry Sauce
A sauce for all occasions

Makes enough for 4:

1 small onion

1 tablespoon butter

1 tablespoon yellow curry paste (or 2 tablespoons curry powder)

1/2 cup dry white wine

1/2 cup chicken stock

3/4 cup heavy cream

Salt, freshly ground pepper

Lemon juice

1 Peel and mince the onion. In a wide saucepan or skillet, melt the butter over medium-low heat. Add the onion and sauté until translucent.

2 Stir in the curry paste (or powder), and mix it well with the melted butter and onion. Pour in the wine, turn up the heat to medium, and let the mixture bubble for a few minutes. Pour in the stock and cream. Let the sauce bubble, uncovered, until it's smooth and creamy, stirring occasionally so that nothing sticks to the bottom of the pan.

3 After 10-15 minutes, when the sauce has a good texture, season it with salt, pepper, and lemon juice to taste. That's it!

Prep time: 25 minutes
Good with: grilled chicken breasts, steamed fish, rice and vegetables, noodles
Calories per serving: 190

Variation:

Hot Curry Sauce
Of course, the type of curry you use determines how hot the sauce is, so watch what you're buying! If you want really hot stuff, sauté 1/4-1/2 teaspoon red chile flakes, some garlic, and chopped fresh ginger with the onions—this will add an exotic Asian flavor. This version's good with rice dishes, with or without meat.

Blue Cheese Sauce
A good, old-fashioned basic

Makes enough for 4:

6 ounces Roquefort or Gorgonzola cheese

3/4 cup milk

Salt, freshly ground pepper

2 tablespoons pine nuts (optional)

1 Cube the cheese, throw it into a heavy saucepan with the milk, and melt it over very low heat. Stir the stuff frequently and never take your eye off the pot. As soon as the sauce is nice and creamy, season it with salt and pepper to taste—that's all there is to this one.

2 A great addition: toast the pine nuts lightly in a dry pan until they start to smell good. Scatter them on top of the sauce.

Prep time: 10 minutes
Good with: pasta, boiled potatoes, steamed vegetables
Calories per serving: 225

Hollandaise
Knock their socks off!

This golden butter sauce can be varied infinitely, and can be spiced up with all the things you love—try some chopped capers, a splash of white wine, a spoonful of mustard, or a sprinkle of minced fresh herbs.

Makes enough for 4:

1 cup butter

4 egg yolks

1 tablespoon water

Salt, freshly ground pepper

3-4 tablespoons fresh lemon juice

1 The first thing to do is get a water bath ready so you don't have to scramble later. Half-fill a large pot with water and turn up the heat until it's bubbling hot (don't boil it, just heat it until tiny bubbles rise to the surface). Find a stainless steel bowl that fits into the pot, but doesn't touch the water.

2 Then, in another pan, slowly melt the butter, skimming off the white foam that rises to the top. It's a good idea to transfer the melted butter to a liquid measuring cup or small pitcher.

3 Put the egg yolks in the metal bowl and whisk with the 1 tablespoon water. Set the bowl in the pan over the hot water. While whisking constantly, slowly drizzle in the melted butter—drop by drop at first, then in a slow stream—and beat well with a whisk. When it looks like a foamy sauce, your job is nearly done—the last step is to add salt, pepper, and lemon juice to taste.

Prep time: 20 minutes
Good with: any vegetable you can think of—but traditionally with asparagus; it's also great with steak, steamed fish, and ham-and-egg-topped English muffins (Eggs Benedict!).
Calories per serving: 430

Dark Meat Stock
Multipurpose and good to have around

Makes 1 quart:

3 tablespoons vegetable oil

Generous 1 pound veal bones (ask the butcher to chop them into small pieces)

1 small leek

3 carrots

4 stalks celery

2-3 onions

2 tablespoons tomato paste

1-2 bay leaves

1 teaspoon peppercorns

1/2 bunch fresh Italian parsley

1 teaspoon salt

1 A large heavy pot (Dutch oven) or roasting pan works best for this. Set it on the stove— over 2 burners if necessary—pour in the oil and turn the heat to high. Throw in the bones and brown them well for 10-15 minutes.

2 Meanwhile, slit the leek lengthwise, wash it well (remember to get between the layers), trim off the root end, and discard any wilted green leaves. Peel the carrots and wash the celery. Chop everything into chunks. Peel and quarter the onions.

3 Once the bones are well browned, add the vegetables to the pan, place it back on the stovetop, and sauté everything together for another 5 minutes. Then, pour off the oil, and put the pot back on the heat. Stir in the tomato paste, and add the bay leaves and peppercorns. Barely cover the contents of the pot with water. Bring the liquid to a boil over high heat, then reduce the heat so that the stock stays at a simmer.

4 Once most of the water has reduced, add more. Repeat the simmering and reducing process—the more you do this, the darker and richer the stock will be.

5 After an hour, wash the parsley and add it to the pot. Simmer for about another hour, remembering to add more water to replace some of the evaporated liquid.

6 Set a big colander on top of another pot, and pour in the entire contents of the stockpot to catch the liquid. Return the stock to the stove and now (not before) add the salt. Skim the fat from the surface or soak it up with paper towels. Cool and refrigerate.

Prep time: 2½ hours

Light Meat Stock
Almost cooks itself

Makes 1 quart:

Generous 1 pound veal bones (ask the butcher to chop them into small pieces)

1 small leek

3 carrots

4 stalks celery

2-3 onions

1-2 bay leaves

1 teaspoon peppercorns

1/2 bunch fresh Italian parsley

1 teaspoon salt

1 To make light stock, you need the same ingredients needed to make dark stock— except that everything is simmered together in water without first being browned.

2 Throw the bones and washed, chopped vegetables into a big pot. Add the bay leaves, peppercorns, and washed parsley. Just cover the ingredients with water and bring to a boil. Reduce the heat and simmer with no lid, and top-off with water occasionally to keep the contents of the pot barely covered with liquid.

3 After about 2 hours, pour the contents of the pot through a colander and collect the stock in another pan. Briefly bring the stock to a boil, and add salt to taste. Skim the fat off the surface of the stock, or absorb it with paper towels. Cool and refrigerate.

Prep time: 2½ hours

Basic Tip
Both stocks will keep for about a week in the refrigerator; or for up to several months in the freezer.

Fish

There's more to fish than fish sticks....

For this chapter we mean everything that swims: in saltwater (like tuna), freshwater (like trout) or in both (like salmon). In lakes, oceans, ponds, rivers, and streams. Sometimes even what's in the tank at the fish market.

But many cooks go straight to the freezer to fish for pre-packaged fillets, or breaded fish products.

But there's much more to fish than fish sticks. Or smoked salmon. Or canned tuna.

And sometimes the best fishy things to eat aren't fish at all—like crab, shrimp, mussels, clams, and squid. We really mean everything that lives in water.

Five Fish Fillets

Here's a handy little guide for when you're standing helplessly looking around at the fish counter

Rockfish
• AKA ocean perch, red rock fish, Pacific red snapper (but it's not true red snapper)
• Inexpensive and very versatile, with firm white flesh and a mild, slightly sweet flavor
• Always sold filleted

Salmon
• A game fish that travels between oceans and rivers, though now salmon is mostly farmed. There are two main varieties—Pacific and Atlantic
• Strong, distinctive flavor, pink to red flesh. Comes whole, filleted, as steaks
• Firm, meaty flesh is good for a variety of cooking techniques

Halibut
• Large flatfish, sold filleted
• Flesh is white and quite lean, with a firm texture and mild, not "fishy" flavor
• You can substitute other varieties of fish for halibut, such as turbot, cod, grouper, or haddock

Tuna
• Large fish, comes in many varieties, from albacore (white flesh) to ahi (red flesh)
• Very meaty flesh, but much lower in fat than meat. Comes in loins, fillets, steaks
• Cook it like you would a steak—rare to medium rare will be the most flavorful; more well done can be dry and unappealing

Sea bass
• Sold whole or filleted, depending on type. There are many species of sea bass, the most common being black sea bass
• Mild white, firm flesh with few bones, can be cooked in a variety of ways
• Chilean sea bass, though not really from the sea bass family, is popular on today's restaurant menus

The Fillet
French: filet; Italian: filetto
Spanish: filete

Fillets are:
• boneless, skinless pieces of fish—ideally about 6 ounces per serving
• available fresh or frozen
• fast and easy to cook
• whole for small fish, like trout, or in segments for large fish, like tuna, salmon, halibut, or cod

Fillets have:
• a lot of nutritious protein
• hardly any fat at all, but some oily varieties, like salmon and tuna, contain high amounts of beneficial omega-3 fatty acids
• abundant vitamins and important chemical substances, such as vitamins A, D, E, and B, fluoride, iodine, and phosphorus

Fillets need:
• to be absolutely fresh
• to be kept cold and stored only briefly
• to have their natural flavors shine through in a recipe

Fillets love:
• butter, olive oil, and cream, but also lighter garnishes like vinaigrettes, and salsas
• fresh herbs, such as dill, tarragon, Italian parsley, chives, thyme, and oregano
• a variety of spices, such as curry, ginger, cumin, fennel seeds, and paprika
• mustard, soy sauce, Asian sauces, pesto, wine (even red wine), vinegar, and fresh lemon juice
• capers, anchovies, garlic, and horseradish
• fennel, cucumber, leeks, mushrooms, spinach, tomatoes, and zucchini
• rice and potatoes, even sometimes pasta or noodles
• NOT: cheese, ketchup, sweet things

What's in a name

Any one fish can go by any number of names, depending on the waters in which it was caught, or the region of the world in which it is served. This can be intimidating to Basic cooks. Following are some examples of fish that have aliases:

salmon trout = arctic char
cod = scrod
grouper = giant sea bass, rock cod
mahi mahi = dolphinfish (NOT dolphin!)
ocean perch = rockfish
red rock fish = Pacific red snapper
squid = calamari
whiting = hake
butterfish = Pacific pompano
flounder = grey sole
wahoo = ono
monkfish = anglerfish
moonfish = opah
black cod = sablefish

In order to avoid confusion in your own kitchen, it's better to categorize fish by the texture and flavor of its flesh. Then, you could easily expand your fish recipe repertoire by substituting different types of fish in your recipes. For example, swordfish is firm-textured and meaty, as is tuna. Plug tuna into your favorite swordfish recipe and Voila! Your first original recipe!

In
Fish that doesn't smell fishy • a willingness to try something new—daring to eat raw fish • seared-rare tuna • fish and chips • BBQ'd fish • fish tacos • *Never out of style: fish fillets with mustard sauce, sautéed fish with capers, lemon, and garlic*

Out
Killing the smell of old, stale fish with lemon • frozen fish sticks and breaded fish fillets • too-thick fish carpaccio • tuna caught in drift nets that also catch dolphins • baked deep-frozen calamari rings • *Never fashionable: imitation crabmeat, fast-food fish sandwiches*

Sushi
Do-it-yourself camaraderie

Homework: hand-rolling rice balls, and shaping them with a mat. A bamboo rolling mat from an Asian market works best for this—but you can also make do with a kitchen towel or cloth napkin. Look for any unfamiliar ingredients in an Asian market or specialty foods store.

Makes 8 nigiri sushi (sliced raw fish on rice) and 16 maki sushi (seaweed-wrapped rice with vegetables or fish rolls):

$1\frac{1}{2}$ cups sushi rice (preferably Japanese short-grain rice; if you can't find any, use the Arborio rice that you'd use to make risotto)
$1\frac{1}{4}$ cups water
3 tablespoons unseasoned rice vinegar
Sugar, salt
4 teaspoons wasabi powder (hellishly hot, bright-green Japanese horseradish—look for it in an Asian market)
8 teaspoons water

For the nigiri sushi:

6 ounces super-fresh tuna fillet (or equally fresh salmon fillet—ask for "sushi- or sashimi-grade" at the fish counter)

For the maki sushi:

6 ounces cucumber
4 ounces carrots
3 tablespoons sake (or rice vinegar)
2 tablespoons water
2 sheets nori (dried seaweed)

For garnish:

Fresh chives, chopped green onion, sliced avocado, pickled ginger (look in an Asian market), soy sauce

1 Rinse the rice in a sieve under cold water until the water runs clear. Drain the rice and let it stand in the colander for 30 minutes. Then, transfer the rice to a saucepan, add the 1¼ cups water, and bring the water to a boil. Boil for a minute, then reduce the heat to very low. Cover the pan and let the rice cook for 20 minutes.

2 Remove the rice from the stove and stir well with a wooden spoon. Spread the rice out on a baking sheet to cool quickly.

3 In a saucepan, mix the rice vinegar with 1 tablespoon sugar and 1 teaspoon salt. Quickly bring the mixture to a boil and remove from the heat. Let the mixture cool, then drizzle it over the cooled rice, and mix with a wooden spoon.

4 In a small bowl, mix the wasabi powder with the 8 teaspoons water to make a paste; set aside.

5 Nigiri sushi: if you're going with salmon, use your fingers to search for any little bones (not necessary for tuna) and use tweezers to remove any troublemakers you might find. Trim the edge of the fillet smooth. Then, cut the fish across the grain into 8 equal slices (any remaining fish can be used later in the maki rolls). Spread one side of each piece of fish with a very thin coat of wasabi paste.

6 Shape about half of the rice into little pads: using a tablespoon, divide the rice into 8 small portions. Dip your hands into cold water (you'll be sorry if you don't—the rice will stick to everything!) and make wide, flat pads out of each scoop of rice. Take one piece of fish in one hand, wasabi-side up, lay a rice pad on top, and press together. Turn the whole thing over—now the fish is on top—and press down firmly. Arrange the nigiri on a serving tray.

7 Maki sushi: Peel the cucumber and carrots. Cut the cucumber in half lengthwise and scrape out the seeds with a spoon. Cut both the cucumber and carrots into strips about 2 inches long and 1/4 inch thick.

8 In a saucepan, bring the sake (or vinegar), water, 1/2 teaspoon sugar and 1/4 teaspoon salt to a boil. Add the carrot strips, simmer briefly, then remove the pan from the stove and add the cucumber strips to the hot broth. Let the vegetables cool in the broth.

9 Heat a dry nonstick skillet over medium heat. Lightly toast the nori sheets on one side (not necessary if the nori is already toasted—it'll say so on the package). As soon as you begin to smell the toasted nori, remove it from pan and let cool. Then, using kitchen scissors, cut the sheets in half.

10 Lay one-half nori sheet, shiny-side down, on a bamboo sushi rolling mat, so that the edge facing you touches the edge of the mat. Spread the nori very thinly (!) with wasabi paste. Spread a layer of rice about 1/4-inch thick on top of the wasabi, leaving about a 1/2-inch margin on the top and bottom. About one third the way from the front edge, make a horizontal groove in the rice into which you insert the vegetable strips and/or leftover fish strips.

11 Lift up the bamboo mat and roll up the nori securely, enclosing the filling piece by piece. Press the mat firmly around the roll, then remove. Place the rolls on a cutting board and cut them in half with a sharp knife. Lay both halves next to each other and slice both in half again—this way all the maki rolls will be the same size. Fill, roll, and slice the remaining nori sheets in the same way. Arrange the maki on a serving tray, cut-surface up, with the nigiri.

12 Garnish the sushi platter with chives, green onions, avocado, and pickled ginger. Place the rest of the wasabi paste and the soy sauce on the table and provide little bowls for dipping. Use chopsticks, or better yet, your fingers.

Prep time: 2 hours
Good with: green tea, Japanese beer, sake
Calories per sushi: (nigiri): 100; (maki): 35

Gravlax
Cured salmon fillets–
Simple and luxurious

Feeds 7 guests + 1 host as an appetizer:

1 teaspoon white peppercorns

1/4 cup coarse salt

3 tablespoons sugar

2 fresh salmon fillets with skin (about 2¼ pounds—ideally center-cut fillets because their thickness will be even)

1 bunch fresh dill

1 The first thing to do is to get a dish for the fish—you could use a soufflé dish or a flat bowl. Use a mortar and pestle or peppermill to crush the peppercorns, leaving them as coarse as possible. Combine them with the coarse salt and sugar.

2 Run your fingertips over both salmon fillets, and remove any bones that you detect with tweezers. Sprinkle both sides of the fish evenly with the salt/pepper/sugar mix. Place 1 fillet skin-side down in the dish.

3 Lightly rinse the dill, shake dry well, and finely chop. Scatter 2/3 of the dill over the salmon fillet in the dish, then place the second fillet on top, with the skin-side up. Scatter the rest of the dill on top.

4 Cover the salmon with foil. Place a wooden board on top and weight it—a couple of food cans or a foil-covered brick do the job well. Put the dish in the refrigerator and leave in there for 2 days. Turn the fish over once or twice daily so that both fillets have a chance to cure thoroughly.

5 And that's it! Slicing and serving the fish is actually harder than preparing it. If you have a proper slicing knife you're home free—one with a long narrow, flexible blade that's perfect for slicing really thin servings. But any other long, sharp knife will work, as well.

6 Remove the fillets from the dish and drain well. Place the fillets skin-side down on a cutting board. Now, angle the long knife so that it's almost horizontal to the fish, run the knife through the fish with a long sawing motion, and the result will be impressively thin slices of salmon.

Prep time: 15 minutes working on the fish, and 2 days watching the refrigerator. Slicing time depends on practice!
Good with: lemon wedges, horseradish, mustard sauce (combine Dijon-style mustard with a touch of sugar, white wine vinegar or fresh lemon juice, oil, and chopped fresh dill to taste), thin slices of bread, crispy pan-fried potatoes, or potato pancakes.
Calories per serving: 260

Shrimp in Lettuce Cups
This one's idiotproof!

Feeds 4 as an appetizer:

8 nice, fresh, crisp butter lettuce leaves

1/2 cup plain yogurt

1/4 cup sour cream

2-3 tablespoons fresh lemon juice

Salt, freshly ground pepper

1/2 bunch fresh dill (or 1 bunch fresh chives)

10 ounces small cooked shrimp (peeled)

1 Wash the lettuce leaves and shake well to dry. Lay 2 leaves on each of 4 small dishes.

2 In a bowl, whisk together the yogurt, sour cream, and lemon juice. Add just a tad of salt and pepper. Wash the dill or chives, shake dry, finely chop, and stir half of them into the yogurt sauce.

3 Lightly rinse the shrimp and drain well. Distribute the shrimp evenly on the lettuce. Pour the sauce over the shrimp and scatter the remaining herbs on top.

Prep time: 15 minutes
Good with: crisp baguette
Calories per serving: 115

Fish Fritters
A great addition to a tapas party

Feeds 4 as an appetizer:

2 slices day-old white bread, with the crust removed

12 ounces fish fillets (e.g. cod, haddock, snapper)

1/2 bunch fresh Italian parsley

2 tablespoons fresh lemon juice

1 egg

Salt, freshly ground pepper

1/2 teaspoon ground coriander

1 tablespoon grated lemon zest

Vegetable oil for deep frying

Bread crumbs (optional)

1 Cut up the bread into very fine pieces, then place in a bowl with a tiny bit of cold water until softened. Run your fingertips over the fish fillets and remove any bones you find with tweezers. Cut the fish fillets into small pieces.

2 Wash the parsley, shake dry, and finely chop. Squeeze the moisture out of the bread and puree it with the fish and lemon juice in a regular blender or with a hand blender. Stir the egg evenly into the mixture, then stir in the parsley. Season with salt and pepper, and the ground coriander and lemon zest.

3 In a large saucepan, wok, or deep-sided skillet, get a couple inches of oil really hot. To test the temperature, immerse the handle of a wooden spoon in the oil—if lots of little bubbles come to surface, the oil is hot enough for frying.

4 Now make a little fritter from the fish mixture: run your hands under cold water, then roll a spoonful of the fish puree between the palms of your hands into a ball. Dunk the ball in the hot oil and wait to see what happens next: if the fish ball disintegrates, the mixture is too soft; you'll have to stabilize it by adding bread crumbs. When you get one that holds together, cook it in the hot oil for 3-4 minutes, fish it out with a skimmer, drain it on paper towels, and taste it when it is cool enough to eat. You may want to adjust the seasonings a bit.

5 When you have the mixture ready, make little balls with the rest of the mixture, fry as shown above, and drain on paper towels. If desired, keep them warm in a low oven (200°F). Serve warm.

Prep time: 40 minutes
Good with: mojo, aioli, creamy curry sauce (see pages 94, 97, 136), pickled hot peppers
Calories per serving: 360

Tuna Tartare
Easy and elegant

Ahi can be expensive, but it's worth the price for a special soirée.

Feeds 4 as an appetizer:

8 ounces sushi-grade ahi tuna fillet

1 small red or yellow bell pepper

1/4 bunch green onions

1 small clove garlic

Small piece fresh ginger (half-thumb sized)

1 tablespoon rice wine (or sherry)

1/4 cup soy sauce

1/2 teaspoon toasted sesame oil

Dash of lemon juice

Sesame seeds for garnish

1 Using a large, sharp knife, cut the tuna into tiny cubes, and put them in a bowl. Halve the bell pepper, remove the stem, ribs, and seeds, and wash both halves. Dice the pepper halves into tiny cubes like the fish, and place in the bowl with the fish.

2 Trim and wash the green onions, finely chop, and add them to the bowl. Squeeze the garlic through a press into the bowl. Peel and mince the ginger and add it to the bowl. Add the rice wine (or sherry), soy sauce, sesame oil, and lemon juice, and mix well.

3 Toast some sesame seeds in a dry nonstick skillet until you just smell their aroma. Remove from the heat.

4 When ready to serve, place the tartare in a mound on a serving plate. Sprinkle with the sesame seeds.

Prep time: 20 minutes (tastes better if allowed to stand a while before serving)
Good with: sesame crackers
Calories per serving: 115

Super-Fast Baked Salmon
Truly basic

Feeds 4:

1³/₄ pounds salmon fillets

5 tablespoons olive oil

Salt, freshly ground pepper

1 lemon

1 Preheat the oven to 475°F.

2 With a sharp knife, cut the salmon fillet into 1/4-inch slices. Brush a baking sheet with 2 tablespoons of the olive oil, and lay the salmon fillets on the pan—one next to the other, not on top of each other, otherwise it won't work.

3 Season the fish with salt and pepper to taste, and drizzle with the lemon juice and the rest of the oil.

4 Put the fish on the middle oven shelf and bake for 2-3 minutes, until cooked through. That's it!

Prep time: 12-13 minutes
Good with: small boiled potatoes and a green salad, light dry white wine
Calories per serving: 495

Peppered Fish
An easy, elegant entrée

Feeds 8:

4 cloves garlic

1¹/₂ lemons

8 pieces fish fillet (about 6 ounces each, e.g., rockfish, sea bass, halibut, cod)

Salt, freshly ground pepper

1/2 cup butter, softened

3 tablespoons brandy

3 teaspoons green peppercorns (drained)

4 tablespoons olive oil

8 tablespoons bread crumbs

1 Peel and press the garlic, and squeeze the juice from the half-lemon. Season the fish lightly with salt, then sprinkle with the garlic and the lemon juice.

2 Preheat the oven to 400°F. In a bowl, mix the butter with the brandy and peppercorns, and season to taste with salt and pepper.

3 Brush a baking sheet with olive oil, and place it in the hot oven to preheat. When it's hot (use an oven mitt!), pull it out again and lay the fish on it in a single layer. Put the tray on the middle oven shelf and bake for about 5 minutes.

4 Pull the pan out of the oven and turn the fish over. Scatter the bread crumbs and little dabs of pepper butter over each fillet. Bake the fish for another 6-8 minutes, until it's cooked through. Cut the remaining lemon into slices and serve with the fish.

Prep time: 30 minutes
Good with: green salad, French bread
Calories per serving: 560

Fish Fillets with Lemon-Caper Butter
A tangy treat

Feeds 4:

1³/₄ pounds fish fillets (e.g., rockfish, sea bass, halibut, cod)

Salt, freshly ground pepper

1/2 bunch fresh Italian parsley

1 lemon

1-2 tablespoons olive oil

3 tablespoons flour

3-4 tablespoons cold butter

1 tablespoon capers (drained)

Sole in Saffron Cream Sauce
Perfect for a quiet evening in

Feeds 4:

1¼ pounds sole (or flounder) fillets

3-4 tablespoons fresh lemon juice

Salt, freshly ground pepper

2 shallots

1 tablespoon butter

1¼ cups fish stock

1/2 cup heavy cream

1/8-1/4 teaspoon crumbled saffron threads

2-3 tablespoons water

1 Season the fillets lightly with salt and pepper. Wash, shake dry, and finely chop the parsley. Wash the lemon with hot water, dry, and grate the zest—then squeeze the juice.

2 In a large nonstick skillet, heat the oil over medium-high heat. Put the flour on a plate, coat both sides of the fish with the flour, and shake off the excess.

3 Lay the fillets in the hot pan and pan-fry for 1 minute. Then, turn down the heat to low, carefully turn the fillets, and pan-fry for another 2-4 minutes, until the fish is no longer translucent. Remove the fish from the pan, cover, and keep warm.

4 Pour the oil out of the pan and wipe the pan lightly with a paper towel. Add the lemon juice and, using a wooden spoon, stir in small dabs of the cold butter. Now, mix in the lemon zest, capers, and parsley. Season with salt and pepper to taste. Put the fillets back in pan briefly to reheat.

Prep time: 30 minutes
Good with: boiled new potatoes
Calories per serving: 265

1 Drizzle the fillets with 2 tablespoons of the lemon juice, and season lightly with salt and pepper. Peel and mince the shallots. Now, set a big rimmed skillet on the stove (the correct lid should be close at hand) and melt the butter over medium heat. Stir in the shallots and sauté until translucent.

2 Pour the stock into the pan. Bring the liquid just to a boil, then immediately turn down the heat so the liquid is quietly bubbling along.

3 Place half of the fillets in the pan and cook, covered, for 2-3 minutes. Carefully transfer the fish to a serving dish, and cover to keep warm. Sauté the rest of the fillets in the same way and keep them warm.

4 Quickly stir the cream into the cooking broth. Dissolve the saffron in the water and add it to the pan. Let the sauce cook away nicely for 2 minutes, until it becomes very creamy. Season the sauce with salt and pepper to taste, and the rest of the lemon juice. Briefly lay the fish in the hot sauce to heat through and serve.

Prep time: 30 minutes
Good with: rice, arugula salad
Calories per serving: 400

Basic Tip
Here's a really good take on cafeteria food

Fried Fish Fillets
Pat four 6-ounce fish fillets (rockfish, sea bass, halibut, cod, haddock) dry with a paper towel. Drizzle them with lemon juice and season with salt and pepper. Dust the fillets lightly with flour and shake off the excess. Then, coat both sides with beaten egg and, finally, coat with bread crumbs. Press the bread crumbs firmly into the fish. Heat 5-6 tablespoons vegetable oil in a large skillet and pan-fry the fillets over medium heat for 3-4 minutes per side, until golden brown. Serve with lemon wedges.

Whole Fish Baked in Salt
Have your friends each bring a pound of salt

It may sound strange, but baking fish in salt really brings out the natural flavors of the fish, and it won't leave it tasting too salty. Plan ahead because you'll need a lot of salt—coarse sea salt or kosher salt is best. Make sure your fish is absolutely fresh—its flavors will only be intensified by the cooking method. Salmon trout are like salmon, only they're smaller and slightly milder in flavor.

Cool tip: plan on serving the lemon tart on page 161 for dessert. You'll be able to use the 2 egg yolks leftover from making this recipe—and anyway it tastes just divine after eating the fish.

Feeds 4:

1 large, fresh salmon trout–AKA arctic char–

(or two smaller ones), about 2½ pounds

1 bunch mixed fresh herbs (such as dill,

Italian parsley, basil)

5½ pounds coarse sea or kosher salt

2 egg whites

About 3/4 cup cold water

3 tablespoons butter

1-2 lemons

Freshly ground pepper

1 Though fresh fish has usually been cleaned at the market, rinse it again well under cold running water when you get home. Pat it dry with paper towels.

2 Lightly rinse the herbs and shake dry. Place the herbs inside the fish's belly and close the pocket well, so that only the fish's skin will come in contact with the salt.

3 Preheat the oven to 475°F.

4 Now it's like making sand castles: haul out a large bowl and pour in the salt. Add the egg whites and water and mix thoroughly.

5 Find a baking dish to fit the fish (or you can use a baking sheet piled about 1 inch high with salt). Place the fish in the dish and plaster it thickly all around with the salt "batter," patting it firmly onto the fish—think of burying your little brother in wet sand.

6 Stick the fish in the oven on the middle shelf and bake for about 30 minutes. Then turn the oven off, and keep the door slightly ajar. Let the fish stand there in its salt jacket for another 10 minutes.

7 In a little saucepan, melt the butter. Cut the lemons into wedges and put them on the table.

8 With a mallet, or similar tool, carefully break open the hard salt crust and free the super-delicate, super-flavorful fish from its salt jacket. You'll want to remove the salt-encrusted skin, too. But the juicy, flavorful fish itself is amazing—serve a piece on a warm plate for each guest. Now it's every man and woman for themselves with the hot butter, fresh lemon juice, or a sprinkling of freshly ground pepper.

Prep time: 1 hour
Good with: potatoes, salad greens, dry white wine
Calories per serving: 465

Asian-Flavored Trout in Foil
A low-fat, ethnic treat

Feeds 4:

4 whole trout (about 9 ounces each)

Salt

3 carrots

1 piece fresh ginger (thumb sized)

4 cloves garlic

2 stalks celery

4 green onions

1/4 cup olive oil

2 limes

1/4 teaspoon chili powder

2 tablespoons sake (rice wine)

1/4 cup soy sauce

1 Rinse the trout inside and out under cold water and set it on a paper towels to dry. Lightly salt the outside and inside of the fish.

2 Peel the carrots, ginger, and garlic. Wash the celery and onions, then chop off any dry or wilted parts. Chop the carrots, celery, and onions into matchstick strips, and mince the ginger and garlic.

3 Preheat the oven to 400°F. Tear off 4 big sheets of aluminum foil and lay them shiny-side up on the work table. Brush the sheets with 1-2 tablespoons of the oil.

4 Squeeze the juice from 1 lime. Heat the rest of the oil in a little saucepan, stir in the chili powder, and toast it for a couple of seconds in the oil. Then, pour in the sake, lime juice, and soy sauce; whisk everything well and remove the pan from the stove.

5 Place each trout on a separate piece of foil. Drizzle the fish inside and out with the soy sauce mixture. Stuff each fish with some of the chopped vegetables, garlic, and ginger and distribute the rest around and on top of each fish.

6 Fold the aluminum foil around each fish to make tightly sealed little packages. Using a skewer or fork, prick the top of each package to let the steam escape. Place the packets on the middle oven shelf and bake for 30 minutes (put a pan underneath to catch drips).

7 Open the foil packages carefully so that the juices don't run out. Lay the fish in individual shallow bowls or plates and drizzle with the cooking juices. Cut the other lime into eighths and serve with the trout.

Prep time: 1 hour
Good with: rice, green tea
Calories per serving: 280

Steamed Lemon Fish
Good and healthy

For this you'll need a wide pan or wok with a lid that seals well. And a sieve or steamer basket that fits the pan so that you can still fit the lid on tightly.

Feeds 4:

1½ pounds halibut or sea bass fillets

Salt, freshly ground pepper

2 lemons

1/2 bunch fresh Italian parsley

1 cup water

14 ounces baby spinach

7 ounces small white mushrooms

1/4 cup good olive oil

1 Rinse the fillets and dry well with paper towels. Cut the fish into 1-inch strips, and sprinkle lightly with salt and pepper.

2 Wash the lemons under hot water and dry. Grate the zest, then halve the lemons and squeeze the juice. Wash the parsley, shake dry, finely chop, and mix with the lemon zest. Put the lemon juice in a saucepan along with the water.

3 Wash the spinach in lots of cold water, and drain in a colander. For the heck of it, wash it again—spinach can be very gritty. If the spinach still has hard little stems attached, just break them off. Using a large knife, coarsely chop the spinach leaves on a big cutting board and place them inside the steamer basket. Wipe the mushrooms clean, discard the little feet, finely slice the caps, and lay them on top of the spinach.

4 Now, lay the fish strips on the spinach bed and scatter over the lemon zest-parsley mixture. Drizzle with 2 tablespoons of the olive oil. Set the steamer basket in the pan and cover with the lid. Bring the lemon water to a boil and, for about 5 minutes (count from when it starts to boil), cook the fish and vegetables over high heat.

5 Divide the fish and vegetables among warm serving plates, season with salt and pepper, and drizzle the fish with the rest of the olive oil.

Prep time: 45 minutes
Good with: steamed parslied potatoes
Calories per serving: 260

Crab Cakes
Easy and tasty

Feeds 4:

1 medium onion

1 small green or red bell pepper

1/4 cup butter

1 pound crabmeat

1/3 cup dried bread crumbs (plus more for dredging)

1/2 cup mayonnaise (plus more if needed)

1½ teaspoons Dijon-style mustard

Splash of Worcestershire sauce

Splash of Tabasco sauce

1½ teaspoons fresh lemon juice

Salt, freshly ground pepper

1/4 bunch fresh Italian parsley

1 lemon

1 Peel and finely chop the onion. Wash and halve the bell pepper, remove the stems, ribs, and seeds, and finely chop.

2 In a skillet, melt 2 tablespoons of the butter over medium heat. Add the onion and pepper and sauté until the onion is translucent. Transfer the mixture to a bowl.

3 Add the crab to the bowl. Add 1/3 cup bread crumbs, the mayonnaise, and mustard, and mix well. Season with the Worcestershire, Tabasco, lemon juice, and salt and pepper to taste. Wash, shake dry, and chop the parsley, then stir it into the crab mixture. If the mixture doesn't hold together well, add a touch more mayonnaise. Refrigerate for about 30 minutes.

4 Form the crab mixture into 8 balls, then flatten the balls to 1/2-inch-thick patties. Dredge the crab cakes in bread crumbs.

5 In a heavy skillet, sauté the crab cakes (in batches if necessary) in the remaining butter over medium heat until golden brown, about 2 to 3 minutes on each side. Serve the crab cakes warm with lemon wedges.

Prep time: 1 hour
Good with: aioli (p 136) or any of the mayonnaise variations (see p 92), Chardonnay, crunchy bread
Calories per serving: 450

Garlic Shrimp
Cocktail party fare

Feeds 4:

1 pound large shrimp

2 cloves garlic

1/2 bunch fresh Italian parsley

8 ounces cherry tomatoes

3 tablespoons butter, melted

1 sprig fresh rosemary

Salt, freshly ground pepper

1 Cut the shrimp along their bellies (use kitchen scissors!) and peel off the shells. With a small knife, slit the shrimp along their backs and remove the dark vein (tip: rinse out the vein under running water).

2 Preheat oven to 400°F. Peel the garlic, wash and shake dry the parsley, and chop both. Wash and halve the tomatoes.

3 In a skillet, melt the butter over medium heat. Sauté the shrimp on both sides for 1-2 minutes. Transfer them to an ovenproof dish. Mix the garlic, tomatoes, parsley, and rosemary in with shrimp, and drizzle with the butter. Bake for about 8 minutes.

Prep time: 30 minutes
Good with: crusty bread, white wine
Calories per serving: 180

113

Mussels or Clams Steamed in Wine
Seems fancy, but it's really easy!

Mussels sometimes come with little hairy whiskers attached to the shells. Be sure to pull off these "beards" when you're cleaning them so you won't gross-out your guests.

Feeds 4:

5½ pounds fresh mussels or clams

1 onion

3-4 cloves garlic

1 red chile pepper (fresh or dried)

3 cups dry white wine

1 bay leaf

Salt, freshly ground pepper

Lots of good crusty bread

1 Rinse the mussels or clams, and, if very dirty, scrub with a vegetable brush. Discard any opened ones.

2 Peel the onion and garlic and coarsely chop. If using a fresh chile pepper, halve it lengthwise, remove the stem, rinse out the seeds, and finely mince. (If using a dried chile, crumble or chop it.)

3 In a huge pot with a tight-fitting lid, bring the wine to a boil with the onions, garlic, chile, bay leaf, and sprinkling of salt and pepper.

4 Throw in the mussels or clams, cover the pot, and wait for a few minutes. Occasionally peek into the pot and remove any opened shellfish—a pair of tongs is best for this job, if you have some. Repeat this process until about 10 minutes have elapsed. After that, throw out any shells that refuse to open and get the rest to the table in a big bowl, with the cooking broth.

5 You don't need tiny shellfish forks for serving—improvise your own using the first victim: pick one mussel or clam out of its shell and pop it in your mouth. Then, use the empty shell like tweezers to wiggle the rest from their houses. Remember to provide extra bowls for each guest to put the empty shells while eating.

6 The best part: dunk the bread in the broth that's left-over after all of the shellfish has been eaten.

Prep time; 25 minutes
Good with: white wine
Calories per serving: 200

Fried Calamari
Make your favorite bar food at home

Feeds 4-6 as a snack:

1 pound fresh or frozen squid bodies

Salt, freshly ground pepper

2 tablespoons fresh lemon juice

2 tablespoons olive oil

2 eggs

1 cup flour

1/2 cup sparkling water

About 2 cups vegetable oil for frying

2 lemons

1 If you're using frozen squid, thaw it in advance. Bring 2 quarts of salted water to a boil in a big pot. Throw in the squid bodies and boil for 1 minute. Drain through a colander, rinse under cold water, and dry well with paper towels.

2 Using a sharp knife, cut the squid bodies crosswise into 1/2-inch strips. Place them in a bowl with a little salt and pepper, the lemon juice, and olive oil, and let stand for a couple minutes (or a couple of hours).

3 Separate the egg whites from the yolks. Place the yolks in a bowl and whisk well with the flour, a pinch of salt, and the sparkling water. Let the mixture stand for about 15 minutes. In another bowl, whip the egg whites until they form stiff peaks. With a big spoon, gently stir the egg whites into the batter, but don't beat for too long and don't try to make batter too even.

4 In a large saucepan (or a wok or deep-fryer if you have one) get the oil really hot—use the wooden spoon trick on page 107 to test the heat.

5 One by one, sweep the calamari rings through the batter so that lots of batter sticks to them. Dunk the battered portions into the hot oil right away.

6 Fry the squid until golden brown, moving them around in the oil occasionally with a cooking spoon so that each one gets done properly. They don't take long: after 2-3 minutes they're done (if they get too done they'll become chewy and unappealing). Fish out the squid with a skimmer and set on a few layers of paper towels to drain. Sprinkle the fried squid with salt, if desired, and eat right away while they're fresh and hot—have the lemon wedges ready for sprinkling to taste.

Prep time: 50 minutes
Good with: tzatziki (p 90), aïoli (p 136), or any type of homemade mayo (p 92)
Calories per serving: 500

Meat
Poult

From meatballs to roast lemon chicken. To each his own....

&
ry

Inside this chapter you'll find a range of basic meat and poultry recipes: chile con carne, braised beef rolls, lemon-chile chicken wings, sweet and sour pork, chicken curry, pan-fried beef fillets, herb-crusted leg of lamb, and more.

If you're not tempted by any of this stuff, don't get mad—just skip to page 133 and read on from there.

For the rest of you: turn the page.

Brisket or Fillet?

Different thicknesses of meat take different times to cook. Sounds logical enough. But it's not that simple. Here's an example: take two equal-sized pieces of beef—one from the tenderloin, and one from the brisket. Now broil both for the same amount of time, and you end up with very different results. The fillet will be tender and delicious, while the brisket will be tough, stringy, and unappealing. Why?

Tender cuts of meat—from parts of the animal that don't get much exercise—can be cooked with dry heat cooking methods, such as quick roasting, sautéing, grilling, and broiling. In these cuts of meat the muscle fibers are finely textured. Tough cuts of meat—from very active parts of the animal—should be cooked with moist-heat cooking methods, (such as braising) and over long periods of time, (such as in slow-roasting) in order to tenderize their tough muscle fibers.

About Slow Roasting and Braising

How do you know whether to slow roast or braise? Here's a quick guide:
Beef: for slow roasting—chuck roast, shoulder roast, rump roast, top round, eye of round, bottom round, top sirloin; for braising—chuck or round (pot roast), brisket, skirt, flank, stew meat
Pork: for slow roasting—Boston butt, crown roast, boneless leg, ham; for braising—shank, shoulder
Lamb: for slow roasting—rib roast, leg, loin roast; for braising—shank, shoulder
Poultry: for slow roasting—whole bird, large breasts (bone-in); for braising—legs and thighs

About Quick Roasting

Typically small, lean, tender cuts are used for quick roasting. Following are some specifics:

Beef: fillet, New York strip, burgers

Pork: rib and loin chops, tenderloin, ham steak, spare ribs

Lamb: rib and loin chops, loin, rack

Poultry: all main parts; breasts cook more quickly than legs/thighs

Of course when in doubt, ask your butcher or follow a trusted recipe.

The Steak

More of a state of mind than a specific type of meat

Steak is:
• a boneless portion of meat or poultry—even fish (but that's another chapter)

• a tender cut, usually cooked with a dry-heat cooking method
• beef: filet mignon, strip, Delmonico, New York, T-bone, porterhouse
• pork: medallions, boneless chops
• lamb: boneless chops, shoulder and leg steaks
• turkey: medallions cut from the boneless breast and thigh

Steak has:
• about 150 calories per 4 ounces (turkey), 300 calories per 4 ounces (beef), and 200 calories per 4 ounces (pork)
• a lot of protein
• plenty of vitamin B complex vitamins and iron

Steak needs:
• to be cut thickly and evenly
• to be stored in a cool and airy place
• to be brought to room temperature before being cooked
• to be cooked without being boiled or burnt
• to be turned with a spatula or tongs rather than a fork
• to be tender even if cooked to well-done
• to rest for a couple of minutes before slicing or serving

Steak loves:
• oil or other cooking fat that can stand high temperatures
• spicy sauces made from the cooking juices
• to be served cold with tasty sauces and dips
• a seared crust
• crispy side dishes
• a fresh salad as a companion

How do you Know When it's Done?

There's definitely an art to pan-frying steaks. We cover the basics on page 27. Here we're helping you to become a master. The test: cooking a 1-inch-thick sirloin steak to the perfect doneness.

Blue (very red, cold in the middle)
Sear for 1 minute, let rest for 2 minutes, pan-fry both sides for another 2-3 minutes, let stand for 2 minutes

Rare (very red, barely warm in the middle)
Sear for 1 minute, let rest for 2 minutes, pan-fry both sides for another 3-4 minutes, let stand for 2 minutes

Medium rare (reddish pink, warm in the middle)
Sear for 1 minute, let rest for 2 minutes, pan-fry both sides for another 4-6 minutes, let stand for 2 minutes

Medium (pink)
Sear for 1 minute, let rest for 2 minutes, pan-fry both sides for another 6-8 minutes, let stand for 2 minutes

Well-done (no trace of pink)
Sear for 1 minute, let rest for 2 minutes, pan-fry both sides for another 10 minutes, let stand for 2 minutes

Exceptions
Filets take 1 minute less. And for each 1/2 inch of thickness, cook the steaks for about 1 minute longer.

Doneness Temps

	rare	med-rare	med	med-well	well
Beef	135°F	140°F	145°F	155°F	160°F
Lamb	135°F	140°F	145°F	155°F	160°F
Pork	—	—	160°F	165°F	170°F
Chicken	—	—	—	—	170°F

In
Lots of buddies and a huge BBQ • remembering your vegetarian friends with an alternative dish • meat in stir-fries • organic bacon • gourmet hamburger patties • eating chicken and turkey legs instead of always the breasts • creative cutlets • a bit of fat for flavor • less meat, more flavor • *Always fashionable: roast chicken, beef stew*

Out
Enemies crashing your BBQ • spoiling others' enjoyment of meat • unidentifiable meat • breaded hamburgers • only eating white meat • having to chew and chew and chew • picking your teeth • *Never in style: meat at all costs, saving the best part for Dad*

Let's have a Barbecue

Though we're all trying to cut down on fat in our diets, don't choose the leanest meat or poultry when you plan on grilling it. Because only meat with enough fat can stand the heat of the coals long enough. Fattier cuts naturally need little help, less fatty cuts can be brushed with oil or wrapped with strips of bacon. A well-marbled sirloin (i.e., streaked with fat) steak cooks medium-rare pretty quickly and can be cooked over a high heat with little added fat.

Preparing meat for grilling:
Remove the meat from the refrigerator 1 hour before cooking. Trim the fat to leave 1/8 inch, even less if it's heavily marbled. Start grilling in a very hot spot, then move to a cooler place to cook through. Let the meat rest for a few minutes at the edge of the grill before serving. Remember: the thicker the meat and the longer the cooking time, the further it needs to be from the heat in order to cook through without burning. Say about 4 inches away for chicken legs, 2½-3 inches for steak and kebabs.

Aiming for Accuracy
With the increased concern over food safety in this country, health authorities recommend using an instant-read thermometer (available in a kitchenware store) to test meats and poultry for doneness, and to cook things to at least medium doneness. On the left is a chart with the corresponding temperatures. Remember to keep the thermometer away from the bone.

Meatballs, Ground Meat Patties, Hamburgers...
Whatever!

Feeds 4:

1 stale roll

2 onions

2 cloves garlic

1/2 bunch fresh Italian parsley

1 tablespoon olive oil

Generous 1 pound mixed ground meat (beef, pork, turkey, or a combination)

2 eggs

1 tablespoon grated lemon zest

Salt, freshly ground pepper

1 teaspoon sweet paprika

1/2 teaspoon dried marjoram

1 tablespoon hot mustard (or ketchup)

Bread crumbs (optional)

1 tablespoon vegetable oil

1 Thinly slice the roll, then cover with hot water to soften it. Peel and finely chop the onions and garlic. Wash and shake dry the parsley, and chop it as finely as possible.

2 Heat the olive oil in a skillet over medium heat and quickly sauté the onion, garlic, and half of the parsley, until the onion is translucent. Remove from the heat and let cool a little.

3 Put the ground meat in a bowl. With your hands, squeeze the excess moisture from the softened roll and add it to the bowl with the ground meat. Add the eggs and the onion-parsley mixture, and mix thoroughly with your hands—the better the mix, the better the meat will hold together during cooking. Mix in the lemon zest and season well with salt and pepper, the paprika and marjoram. Mix in the mustard (or ketchup). Mix in the remaining fresh parsley.

4 Douse your hands in cold water and make small or medium-sized balls with the meat mixture (from ping pong ball- to tennis ball-sized). Keep your hands wet to prevent sticking. If the mixture is still too loose to mold, mix in a couple of spoonfuls of bread crumbs. If you're making patties or hamburgers, flatten the balls and lay them next to one another on a plate.

5 In a large skillet, heat the oil over medium heat and brown the meatballs or patties. Turn them to brown the other side and cook through. For patties, it'll take 5-7 minutes per side, depending on size. Meatballs will take 10-15 minutes. Serve immediately—delish!

Prep time: 1 hour
Good with: mustard, ketchup, horseradish, pickles, French fries, beer
Calories per serving: 530

Variations:

Mediterranean Meatballs
Combine the ground meat with the softened roll and eggs, as directed above. Season with lots of chopped fresh garlic, freshly ground pepper, basil, some squirts of lemon juice, and 1-2 small spoonfuls of tomato paste. Form small meatballs from the mixture and flatten them just slightly. Fry the meatballs in 1 tablespoon of olive oil. When nearly done, add 1 teaspoon butter to the pan for an even crispier exterior. These are good with or without pasta, with a thick, aromatic tomato sauce, French bread, and a glass of red wine.

Asian Meatballs
With your hands, mix a generous pound of ground beef with 1 egg, then add finely chopped fresh ginger, garlic, and green onions to taste—be bold! Season with some grated lemon zest and 1/4-1/2 teaspoon *sambal oelek* or other hot chile paste, and salt and pepper to taste. Form little balls from the mixture and flatten them just slightly. Cook the meatballs in lightly boiling salted water for 10-15 minutes. Drain, then toss them in a skillet with some oil for a couple of minutes to crisp the outsides.

Chili Con Carne
A football party staple

Feeds 4-6:

2-3 onions

3 cloves garlic

2-3 carrots

2 stalks celery

1 small red bell pepper

1 small green bell pepper

1 large can peeled tomatoes (28 ounces)

1/4 cup vegetable oil

Generous 1 lb lean ground beef

2 cups meat stock (or 1 cup stock + 1/4 cup full-bodied red wine)

1 tablespoon fresh oregano leaves

1/2-1 teaspoonful *sambal oelek* or other hot chile paste

Salt, freshly ground pepper

1 can kidney beans (15 ounces)

1 Peel and finely chop the onions and garlic. Peel the carrots. Wash and trim the celery. Wash and halve the bell peppers, and remove the stems, ribs, and seeds. Dice all of the fresh vegetables as finely as possible. Coarsely the chop the canned tomatoes.

2 Set a large, heavy pot on the stove and add the oil. Turn the heat to medium-high. First, sauté the ground beef by itself until it is brown and crumbly. Then, mix in the onions and garlic and sauté together briefly. Next, throw in the carrots, celery, and peppers, and sauté for a couple of minutes. Last of all, add the tomatoes with their juice.

3 Now pour in the stock (or the stock plus wine), and season with the oregano, *sambal oelek*, and salt and pepper to taste. Bring the mixture to a boil, then cover and simmer over medium heat for 1-1½ hours.

4 Pour the canned beans into a colander and rinse them. Into the pot they go—and let the stew bubble along for another 15 minutes. Don't forget to season to taste with salt and pepper and make it nice and hot.

Prep time: busy 45 minutes, relaxing 1¾ hours
Good with: cornbread, grated cheese, chopped onions, sour cream
Calories per serving (6): 345

Beef Rolls
This is comfort food

Feeds 4:

4 thin slices beef round (5-6 ounces each–ideally, ask your butcher to pound them thinly)

Salt, freshly ground pepper

4 teaspoons hot mustard

8 thin slices smoked bacon

1 large dill pickle

2 onions

1 tablespoon flour

1 carrot

2 stalks celery

1/4 cup vegetable oil

2 tablespoons tomato paste

1/2 cup dry red wine

1½ cups meat stock

Pinch of cayenne pepper

1 Lay the beef slices on a cutting board and season lightly with salt and pepper. Spread each slice thinly with mustard and place 2 slices of bacon on each slice. Cut the pickle into fine strips and distribute them on top of the bacon. Peel and halve 1 of the onions, cut it into thin slices, and divide the slices among each portion.

2 To roll, first fold the longer sides of the beef slices inward, then roll the shorter sides up around the filling into tight cylinders. Secure the rolls with toothpicks. Dust the beef rolls with flour and shake off the excess.

3 Peel and dice the second onion and the carrot. Trim the celery, then wash and chop into tiny cubes.

4 Pull out a casserole dish or a heavy pan with a lid that fits. Add the oil and place over medium-high heat. Place the rolls in the pan and brown on all sides. Season the rolls with salt and pepper and transfer them to a plate.

5 Throw all of the diced vegetables into the pan, stir them into the pan drippings, and sauté over medium heat until the onions are translucent. Stir in the tomato paste, pour in the red wine, and crank up the heat. Now, pour in the stock and place the rolls in the pan. When the liquid comes to a boil, turn the heat way down to low, cover the pan, and simmer the rolls for about 1 hour.

6 Remove the rolls from the pan and put them on a plate. Bring the sauce to a boil and stir well. Season generously with salt and pepper to taste, and the cayenne pepper. Return the rolls to the pan and heat through.

Prep time: busy 45 minutes, relaxing 1 hour
Good with: mashed potatoes or noodles
Calories per serving: 500

Lemon-Chile Chicken Wings
Don't forget the napkins!

Feeds 4 as a snack:

12 chicken wings, as meaty as possible

1 sprig fresh rosemary

4-5 tablespoons lemon juice

1 heaping tablespoon honey

1 tablespoon ketchup

1 teaspoon Worcestershire sauce

1/4-1/2 teaspoon red chile flakes

Salt, freshly ground pepper

1 Rinse the chicken wings under cold water and pat dry well with paper towels. Remove the leaves from the rosemary sprig and finely chop. Place the the rosemary in a bowl with the lemon juice, honey, ketchup, and Worcestershire sauce, and whisk well. Add the chile flakes. Season the marinade generously with salt and pepper.

2 Place the chicken wings in a bowl, pour the marinade over the top, and stir to coat the wings well with the marinade. Cover the bowl and chill until ready to put on the grill.

3 Remove the wings from the marinade and put them on a medium-hot charcoal grill.

Grill the wings, turning to cook both sides, for 10 to 15 minutes, until they're cooked through and crispy.

(Foul weather alternative: cook the wings under the broiler—don't forget to turn them!)

Prep time: 15 minutes, plus BBQ time
Good with: beer!
Calories per serving: 375

Sweet & Sour Pork
Let's wok, baby!

Feeds 4:

1¼ pounds lean pork cutlets

1 leek

1/2 cucumber

1 piece fresh ginger (thumb sized)

3-4 cloves garlic

2 tablespoons sugar

1/4 cup rice vinegar

3-4 tablespoons soy sauce

1/4 cup sake (or dry sherry)

2 teaspoons cornstarch

1 tablespoon tomato paste

Cayenne pepper

6 tablespoons vegetable oil

1 Halve the cutlet lengthwise, then cut it crosswise into small pieces.

2 Discard any wilted parts of the leek and cut off the root end. Slit the leek lengthwise and wash it under running water—remember to get the sand out from between the inner layers. Cut the leek into very fine slices. Peel the cucumber, cut it in half lengthwise, scrape out the seeds, and cut it into slices. Peel and chop the ginger and garlic.

3 Now prepare the sauce: whisk together the sugar, vinegar, soy sauce, sake (or sherry), cornstarch, and tomato paste. Season to taste with a little or a lot of cayenne pepper.

4 Put a wok or large skillet on the stove, get it really hot, and pour in the oil. First, stir-fry the meat strips for 1 minute. Then, push the meat to edge of the pan and throw in the leek, ginger, and garlic; stir-fry briefly. Mix in the meat and the cucumber, then pour in the sauce and bring to boil. Simmer gently for about 1 minute, stirring until the sauce thickens and coats the ingredients.

Prep time: 35 minutes
Good with: rice
Calories per serving: 350

Chicken Curry
Asian cooking 101

Feeds 4:

1 piece fresh ginger (thumb sized)

1 small onion

2 cloves garlic

1 lemon

1 tablespoon curry paste (look in an Asian foods store or in the international section at the supermarket)

4 boneless skinless chicken breast halves (about 6 ounces each)

2 tablespoons vegetable oil

2-3 tablespoons soy sauce

1 can unsweetened coconut milk (14 ounces)

Pinch of sugar

Salt

1 Peel and mince the ginger, onion, and garlic. Grate the lemon zest and squeeze out the lemon juice. Stir everything above together with the curry paste.

2 Cut the chicken breasts into 1/2-inch strips. Get a wok of large skillet hot, and add the oil. Stir in the chicken strips, brown well all over, and remove from the pan.

3 Pour off the cooking fat, leaving just a thin film in the pan. Add the soy sauce and scrape up the browned bits from the bottom of the pan. Separate the thick, creamy cap from the top of the coconut milk, stir half of it into the pan, and set the rest aside.

4 Now, stir the curry paste mixture into the pan. Simmer the mixture over low heat for 1-2 minutes, stirring constantly. Stir in the sugar, and gradually add the liquidy coconut milk. Stir in the lemon juice. At the last minute, add the last dollop of coconut cream, then return the chicken to the pan. Season with salt to taste and heat through.

Prep time: 45 minutes
Good with: rice
Calories per serving: 310

Breaded Chicken Cutlets
Easy, but impressive

Feeds 4:

4 boneless chicken breast halves (about

6 ounces each) you can also use turkey or

pork cutlets, or even veal cutlets—very

German!

3 tablespoons flour

2 eggs (lightly beaten)

About 1 cup bread crumbs

Salt, freshly ground pepper

3 tablespoons vegetable oil

1/4 cup butter

1 lemon

1 Rinse the chicken breasts and pat dry with paper towels. Remove the skin (if present). Place each chicken breast between two large pieces of plastic wrap. With a meat mallet (or any other strong, blunt kitchen implement), pound the breasts until they are flat and even in thickness.

2 Pull out three large, shallow dishes. Put the flour in the first one, the eggs in the second, and the bread crumbs in the third.

3 Season the cutlets with salt and pepper. Dredge them in flour and shake off the excess. Dip both sides in egg, then dredge in bread crumbs, turning to coat both sides generously. Don't pat the coating too firmly.

4 In a large skillet, heat the oil over medium heat, add the butter and heat until foamy. Add the chicken cutlets, sauté them on one side until golden brown, then turn and sauté the other side—each side takes about 2-3 minutes. Cut up the lemon and put a wedge on each plate.

Prep time: 30 minutes
Good with: cucumber salad, potatoes
Calories per serving: 400

Chicken Saltimbocca
The flavors jump in your mouth

Feeds 4:

4 boneless chicken breast halves (about

6 ounces each)

8 thin slices prosciutto

8 medium-sized fresh sage leaves

3-4 tablespoons butter

Salt, freshly ground pepper

1/2 cup dry white wine

1 Cut the chicken breasts in half. Remove the skin (if present). Just like in the previous recipe, you have to flatten the chicken breasts first (see step 1). Top each flattened cutlet with a slice of prosciutto and 1 sage leaf, securing them in place with a toothpick (see photo). In a large skillet (do not use nonstick), melt 2 tablespoons of the butter over medium heat. Throw in the chicken and pan-fry each side for about 2 minutes. Season lightly with salt and pepper.

2 Remove the chicken from the pan and keep warm (cover with aluminum foil). Pour the wine into the pan, bring it to a boil, and—using a spatula—scrape up the browned bits on the bottom of the pan (this is what makes the sauce taste so good). Add the rest of the butter and stir with a whisk until melted. Place the cutlets back in the pan and reheat briefly—and you're done!

Prep time: 25 minutes
Good with: dry Italian white wine, crusty bread, green salad
Calories per serving: 300

Steak with Onions and Wine
Perfect for an intimate dinner...

Feeds 2:

2 small onions

1/2 teaspoon black peppercorns

2 thick beef fillet steaks (about 7 ounces each)

2 tablespoons vegetable oil

2 tablespoons cold butter

Salt

1/2 cup dry red wine

1 Preheat the oven on its lowest setting (180-200°F). Peel and halve the onions and thinly slice. Grind the peppercorns coarsely in a peppermill.

2 Pat the steaks dry with paper towels. In a skillet, heat the oil over medium-high heat until it's very hot. Throw in the steaks and sear them for about 2 minutes, until the underside no longer stubbornly clings to the bottom of the pan. Turn the steaks (do: use a spatula; don't: use sharp prongs).

3 Add 1 tablespoon of the butter to the pan and continue to pan-fry the steaks for another 2, 6, or 8 minutes, depending on

how you like them done inside: almost raw, pink, or cooked through, respectively. Take the steaks out of the pan, and season to taste with salt and pepper. Put them on a plate and keep them warm in the oven.

4 Stir the onions into the hot fat in the pan and sauté them until browned. Add the red wine and bring to a boil. Then, cut the remaining 1 tablespoon butter into little pieces and stir it vigorously into the onions. Lightly season the onion sauce with salt and pepper. Pour the sauce over the steaks.

Prep time: 20 minutes
Good with: Potatoes au Gratin (see p 57), red wine, candlelight...
Calories per serving: 410

Stir-Fried Turkey Tenders
Quick and spicy

Feeds 4:

20 ounces turkey tenders (boneless turkey portions)

1 bunch green onions

3 carrots

1 small red bell pepper

1 piece fresh ginger (thumb sized)

2 tablespoons olive oil

1 teaspoon coriander seeds

1 teaspoon cumin seeds

2 tablespoons fresh lemon juice

1 teaspoon turmeric

1/2-1 teaspoon *sambal oelek*, or other hot chile paste

1/4 cup cashew nuts or peanuts

2-3 tablespoons vegetable oil

Water

1 Cut the turkey tenders into thin strips about 1/2-inch wide.

2 Cut away any wilted parts and the root ends of the green onions. Wash them and shake dry. Cut thicker ones lengthwise, then chop all into 1-inch pieces. Peel the carrots and thinly slice.

3 Wash and halve the pepper. Remove the stem, ribs, and seeds, then coarsely chop the pepper halves. Peel the ginger and chop it a little smaller. Then, mince both with a hand blender or regular blender, and add the olive oil, coriander, and cumin. Puree the mixture, then mix in the lemon juice and turmeric. Spice it up with the *sambal oelek*.

4 Place a wok or large skillet on the stove and heat it, at first with no oil, over medium-high heat. Toss in the nuts and toast them a little, remembering to stir. As soon as they begin to smell good—and in any case before they turn black—get them out of the pan.

5 Now add 1 tablespoon of the oil to the wok, then add the onion and carrot and stir-fry. After 3-4 minutes, push the vegetables to the edge of the wok and pour another 1-2 tablespoons of the oil into the middle. Stir-fry the meat for 1 minute max. Now, mix in the vegetables waiting at the edge of the wok, stir in the pepper sauce, and add a couple of tablespoons of water. Simmer everything together for another 2 minutes. Scatter the toasted nuts on top.

Prep time: 40 minutes
Good with: rice—this one you've gotta eat with chopsticks!
Calories per serving: 325

Hungarian Goulash
Especially good on cold, stormy days

This recipe used to be a secret of a Hungarian cook. Years ago, he made it exclusively for kaisers and kings near the Austro-Hungarian border.

Feeds 4-6:

6 medium onions

3 cloves garlic

2½-2¾ pounds beef stew meat (preferably from the shank)

1/4 cup vegetable oil

5 tablespoons sweet paprika

1 teaspoon dried marjoram

1 teaspoon dried thyme

1 teaspoon caraway seeds

1 tablespoon red wine vinegar

8-10 tablespoons water, plus more as needed

Salt, freshly ground pepper

1 The first thing to do is to peel and dice the onions and garlic. The vertical pictures on the right show how the professionals do it. But chopping works too, if you're not such a perfectionist.

2 Now cut the meat—but not too small. Trim away any bits of fat. You want finger-sized, 1½-inch-long strips.

3 In a heavy pot, heat the oil over medium-high heat. Add the onions and sauté until they are translucent and almost brown—but only almost!

4 Paprika, Take 1: 3 tablespoons of it are quickly sautéed, together with the onion, garlic, marjoram, thyme, and caraway. Then, in goes the vinegar and water.

5 Now add the meat. It's best not to stir it right away, so it can get a little color. But it doesn't have to be pan-fried, like on page 27. In fact it shouldn't be pan-fried at all, so it can get nice and tender.

6 Now add a bit of salt and pepper, stir, and turn down the heat to low. Put the lid on the pot and simmer. You're thinking: Shouldn't I add more liquid? No. The onions and meat should exude plenty of their own natural juices. But keep checking the cooking process occasionally: only when there is almost no liquid left should you add a couple of spoonfuls of water. Keep the stew at a simmer, rather than a boil—otherwise it will dry out. After a good 1½ hours, or perhaps even longer, the meat will be almost done.

7 Paprika, Take 2: stir in the remaining 2 tablespoons paprika and let it cook with the meat for a short while. At this point, barely cover the meat with water. After about 15 minutes of simmering, it should be done, though you'll still need to season to taste before serving.

Prep time: busy 1 hour, relaxing 1½ hours
Good with: boiled potatoes, green salad, or crusty rolls, beer or red wine
Calories per serving (6): 390

Basic Tips

If you and your friends like things hot, you can spice up the goulash by adding hot paprika or cayenne pepper right at the end. Vegetables are a great addition to this meat stew—e.g., small pieces of bell pepper, peeled tomato, or even grated green cabbage. Just throw them into the pot before the lid goes on.

Sherried Chicken
The Spanish sister of
coq au vin

Feeds 2-3:

1 roasting chicken (about 3 pounds) cut into

6 pieces (2 leg-thighs, 2 wings, 2 breasts)

Salt, freshly ground pepper

1 tablespoon sweet paprika

2 onions

1 small red bell pepper

1 small yellow or green bell pepper

2-3 cloves garlic

3 tablespoons vegetable oil

1 cup dry sherry

1/2 cup chicken stock

1 Rinse the chicken pieces, and dry with paper towels. Season the chicken all over with salt and pepper, and rub the pieces with the paprika.

2 Peel and halve the onions, and finely slice. Wash and halve the peppers. Remove the stems, ribs, and seeds, then halve the pepper halves once more and cut them into fine strips. Peel and mince the garlic.

3 In a wide pot with a lid that fits, heat the oil over medium heat. Add the chicken pieces and sauté for about 10 minutes, until browned on all sides. Then add the onions, pepper strips, and garlic, and sauté briefly.

4 Now pour the sherry and stock into the pot and let things simmer away over medium-low heat for about 10-12 minutes. Put the lid on, turn off the stove, and let the stuff stand for another 10 minutes. And that's it! Season to taste with salt and lots of freshly ground pepper.

Prep time: 50 minutes
Good with: bread or rice
Calories per serving (3): 770

Roast Lemon Chicken
Always a classic

Feeds 2-3:

1 roasting chicken (about 3 pounds)

Salt, freshly ground pepper

3 tablespoons olive oil

1 large lemon

2-3 sprigs fresh thyme (or 1 sprig fresh

rosemary)

1 Rinse the chicken under cold water, and dry with paper towels. For now, just season the inside with salt and pepper. Preheat the oven to 425°F. Coat the inside of a casserole dish with 1 tablespoon of the oil.

2 Wash the lemon in hot water and dry. Using a fork, prick the lemon skin from top to bottom and all around several times (so the juice can come out during cooking and give the chicken a fresh tangy taste from inside). Push the lemon inside the chicken cavity, and follow with the washed herb sprigs. Cross the chicken legs over the cavity and tie them together with cotton kitchen string. Now, season the outside of the bird with salt and pepper, and rub it all over with the remaining 2 tablespoons olive oil.

3 Place the stuffed chicken on its side in the casserole, put it in the oven on the second shelf from the bottom, and roast it for 20 minutes. Then, turn the chicken on its other side, and roast it for another 20 minutes. Periodically during roasting, use a spoon to scoop out the cooking juices and baste the chicken with it. Next, turn the bird on its back (breast up) and roast for another 25 minutes, continuing to baste. Now prod a leg with a skewer or small sharp knife—if the juices that run out are still pink, it's not done, and you should continue to roast. Better yet–insert an instant-read thermometer into the meaty part of a thigh (avoid the bone). If done, it should read 170°F. Whisk it out and onto the table for carving!

Prep time: busy 10 minutes, relaxing a good hour (with some interruptions)
Good with: salad and bread
Calories per serving (3): 370

The 175-Degree Duck Breast
Super simple

Feeds 2:

2 duck breasts (about 7 ounces each)

Salt, freshly ground pepper

1 Preheat the oven to 175°F. It's a good idea to check the oven's heat with an oven thermometer—look for one in a kitchenware or specialty foods store.

2 With a sharp knife, score the duck skin diagonally a few times (but don't cut into the meat). Rub it with salt and pepper.

3 Place an ovenproof skillet (i.e., without a plastic handle) on the stovetop over medium-high heat. When hot, place the duck breasts skin-side down in the pan and sear. Turn and quickly sear the other side.

4 Place the pan in the oven—now you've got 30-45 minutes of downtime. Cooking the duck breast over this low heat makes it really tender; the meat turns a uniform delicate pink and is juicy and moist.

5 Remove the duck breast from the pan and let it rest for 5-10 minutes on a cutting board. With a very sharp knife, cut the duck crosswise into very thin slices.

Prep time: busy 10 minutes, kicking back 30-45 minutes
Good with: bread, mango chutney (ready-made or home-made—see page 90)
Calories per serving: 450

Basic Tip

Pan-Roasted Duck Breast—you don't need an oven for this one

Season the duck with salt and pepper. Score the skin diagonally. Heat a nonstick skillet over medium-low heat. Place the duck breasts skin-side down in the pan, cover the pan, and pan-roast the duck for 10 minutes. Turn the duck over and pan-roast for about 10 more minutes, then wrap in aluminum foil and let rest for a few minutes before slicing.

Pork Roast
A crowd pleaser

Feeds 6-8:

2¾-3 pounds boneless pork roast with rind

1 pound pork bones (ask the butcher)

1/2 teaspoon caraway seeds

3 cloves garlic

2 tablespoons vegetable oil

1 teaspoon sweet paprika

Salt, freshly ground pepper

2 onions

2 carrots

1 stalk celery

1 bay leaf

Light beer (optional)

1 Using a sharp knife, score the pork rind in a diamond pattern (don't cut into the meat). Chop the caraway seeds a tad smaller. Peel and mince 1 clove of the garlic. Stir together the caraway, minced garlic, oil, and paprika, and rub the mixture into the roast well. Wrap the meat in foil and let it rest overnight in the refrigerator.

2 At least 3 hours before you plan to eat, preheat the oven to 475°F. Unwrap the pork and season it all over with salt and pepper. Place the pork rind-side down in a large roasting pan. Place the pan on the stovetop and brown on all sides. Take the meat out of the pan, put the bones into the pan drippings, and roast in the oven until the bones are browned. Then, put the pork back in the pan—rind side up.

3 Now, roast the pork in the oven for 30 minutes, occasionally basting the meat with the accumulated pan juices. Peel the onions, carrots, and celery, and cut into small cubes. Peel the remaining cloves of garlic.

4 Turn down the oven heat to 350°F and add all the vegetables, the garlic, and bay leaf to the roasting pan. Pour a shot of water (or light beer) over the meat: now it'll take another 1½ hours until the meat is crispy on the outside and tender on the inside. Baste it now and again with the pan juices, and/or add more water or beer if it seems too dry. When done, it will read 165°F on an instant-read thermometer.

5 Place the roasting pan on top of the stove, transfer the pork to an ovenproof dish, and return it to the oven (now it should be off) to sit until the gravy is ready. Pour the contents of the roasting pan through a sieve into a saucepan. Cook the pan juices so that they reduce and thicken a little. Season the gravy to taste and serve with the sliced pork.

Prep time: Busy 45 minutes, relaxing 3 hours
Good with: potatoes, dumplings
Calories per serving (8): 390

Beef Braised in Red Wine
Very Italian, very tasty

Feeds 4-6:

2 cloves garlic

2¼ pounds braising beef (e.g., brisket, chuck, thick flank—better ask the butcher!)

2 stalks celery

2 carrots

1 onion

3 tablespoons olive oil

2-3 tablespoons butter

Salt, freshly ground pepper

1½ cups dry red wine

2 whole cloves

1 bay leaf

1 small can peeled tomatoes (14.5 ounces)

1 cup meat stock

Freshly ground nutmeg

1 Peel the garlic cloves and cut them into slivers. Then, with the point of a little knife, slit the meat here and there, and poke the garlic pieces into the holes.

2 Wash the celery and chop off any wilted or old parts from. Peel the carrots and onion. Cut all of the vegetables into cubes.

3 Set a large roasting pan (make sure it has a lid that fits) on top of the stove, pour in the olive oil, and heat over medium-high heat. Add the butter and melt it in the hot oil. Now add the meat and brown it on all sides.

4 When the meat is totally browned, add the cubed vegetables to the pan and brown them. Season to taste with salt and pepper, add the wine, and turn up the heat to high. Scatter the cloves and bay leaf in the pan juices.

5 Coarsely chop the tomatoes and add them to the pan juices. Now add the stock, and a touch of nutmeg. Cover the pan, turn the heat to low—and take a break for 3 hours! The roast should be completely left alone to simmer away by itself—but don't let it boil.

6 Before serving, remove the beef from the pan, strain the pan juices (don't use a pasta colander, use a fine mesh strainer, or a conical sieve). Of course, if you like the gravy to have little pieces of vegetables, you can skip the straining part—just remove the bay leaf and cloves. In either case, reheat the gravy and season it to taste with salt and pepper. Serve it with the thinly sliced meat.

Prep time: busy 30 minutes, relaxing 3 hours
Good with: polenta (just follow the instructions on the package), full-bodied Italian red wine
Calories per serving (6): 405

Herb-Crusted Leg of Lamb
One serious roast

Feeds 4-6:

1 lemon

$2\frac{1}{4}$ pounds leg of lamb (boned)

$2\frac{1}{4}$ pounds boiling potatoes

20 ounces ripe tomatoes

6 tablespoons olive oil

Salt, freshly ground pepper

3 tablespoons butter

1 bunch fresh Italian parsley

4 cloves garlic

1/4 cup bread crumbs

2 ounces Parmesan cheese, freshly grated

1 Wash the lemon under hot water, dry it, and grate the zest. Then, cut the lemon in half and squeeze the juice. Rub the leg of lamb with the lemon juice.

2 Wash, peel, and finely slice the potatoes. Bring a quart of water to a boil, and plunge the tomatoes briefly in the water. Rinse the tomatoes under cold water, and remove the skins with a paring knife—after the scalding treatment, it's really easy. Coarsely chop the tomatoes, discarding the stems.

3 Coat the inside of a large roasting pan with 2 tablespoons of the olive oil. Layer the potato slices in the pan, and season them with salt and pepper. Distribute 2 tablespoons of the butter in little pats over the potatoes. Scatter the tomatoes on top. Preheat the oven to 350°F.

4 Wash the parsley, shake dry, and chop as finely as possible. Peel and mince the garlic. Mix the parsley and garlic with the bread crumbs and lemon zest. Stir slightly more than half of this mixture in a small bowl with the remaining 4 tablespoons olive oil to make a paste. Combine the rest with the grated cheese in another bowl.

5 Now season the lamb with salt and pepper. Smear the entire roast with the olive oil paste. Lay the lamb on top of the potato-tomato bed. Roast on the middle oven shelf for $1\frac{1}{4}$ hours.

6 Now turn up the oven temperature to 425°F. Scatter the parsley-cheese mixture over the lamb, and distribute pats of the remaining 1 tablespoon butter on top. Roast for 10-15 minutes, until the crust is brown and crispy. When done, it will read at least 145°F on an instant-read thermometer (medium-rare). Let it rest for a few minutes.

Prep time: busy 45 minutes, relaxing $1\frac{1}{2}$ hours
Good with: Italian red wine
Calories per serving (6): 700

131

Veget

...anything (almost) that grows and is harvested and is eaten

ables

For our purposes, vegetables are anything (almost) that grows and is harvested and is eaten. A vegetable can be the root, the stem, the leaf, the fruit, or even the seeds of a plant.

Wild vegetables were discovered thousands of years ago in China and Egypt. One day, someone came up with the idea of cultivating the things that, up until then, had only been gathered. People didn't start growing vegetables in Europe until almost the end of the Middle Ages.

Vegetables originate from different places throughout the world. The cucumber grew up in India, spinach in the Caucasus, and the radish—common in today's French bistros and German beer gardens—hails from China and Egypt. Central Europe gave us the cabbage and beet, while the Americas, South America specifically, produced the tomato.

Vegetables can be cooked in a ton of ways—they taste great sautéed, steamed, boiled, braised, broiled, baked, and even barbecued.

Read on to discover how to do it.

What's Left after Cleaning?

If you're serving vegetables as a side dish, about 5-7 ounces per person usually arrives on the plate. You'll use twice as much if the veggies are the main meal—that's post-cleaning weight. Remember this when you're shopping: you'll have to buy more than you think you need in order to account for the waste from trimming and cleaning.

The following examples show what's left of 7 ounces (1 portion) of vegetables

Snow Peas
Chop off the ends, strip off the strings—6.65 ounces left

Baby Spinach
Pull off any hard stems, discard any wilted leaves—6.3 ounces left

Asparagus
Cut off the ends, peel the bottom third—5.6 ounces left

Bell Peppers
Remove the stems, ribs, and seeds—5.25 ounces left

Green Onions
Cut off the root ends, cut off the dark green parts and wilted outside leaves—4.9 ounces left

Broccoli
Cut out the core and lop off the thick stems, get rid of any yellowing florets—4.2 ounces left

Leeks
Chop off the root ends, throw away the outer and dark green leaves—3.5 ounces left

To Be or Not to Be...Vegetarian

For years there's been a debate about whether vegetarians are smart or senseless. Now that vegetarians have come out of the root cellar and into the mainstream, it's cool not to eat meat. But, some ask, won't eating

only vegetables make you unhealthy? If your plate is as colorful as the vegetable stand it's unlikely anything bad will happen. Just make sure you're getting enough protein.

There are many types of vegetarians. If you want to start simply, reduce the animal products you eat to just milk, cheese, and eggs—now you're an ovo-lacto-vegetarian. If you exclude eggs, you're a lacto-vegetarian. Green vegetables, sprouts, and nuts can basically give you the important things you'd get from eggs and milk. Some vegetarians don't want to eat anything that is animal in origin—not even honey (comes from bees). And they prefer everything raw—as in no cooking!! These are called vegans. We prefer a more balanced approach.

Cooking up something fresh

You may find it frustrating that all vegetables don't take the same amount of time to cook. Following is a handy table that will help you time your veggies right. Steaming is among the healthiest ways to prepare vegetables, and they'll need only a simple garnish before going onto the plate.

1 minute
Steamed fresh spinach

2 minutes
Steamed sliced zucchini or mushrooms

3−4 minutes
Steamed sliced leeks

5 minutes
Steamed bell pepper squares

8 minutes
Boiled broccoli florets

10−12 minutes
Steamed fennel strips, or boiled green asparagus or cauliflower florets

12−15 minutes
Steamed celery or carrot slices, or boiled green beans

15−20 minutes
Steamed cauliflower florets, or boiled potatoes

The Benefits of Vegetables

Vegetables are healthy, we know that. But not many people realize just how good they are for the body, both inside and out. Here are five vegetables and their attributes, which, when eaten, will make life just a little bit better:

	Body	Beauty	Brain	Bonus
Eggplant	Regulates cholesterol	Makes skin look good	Stimulates mental activity	Combats stress
Beans	Provide muscle power, cleanse the digestive system	Strengthen hair, bones, skin and teeth	Combat nervousness	Give energy
Carrots	Improve vision	Keep eyes and skin looking bright	Feed the brain	Provide strength
Bell Peppers	Strengthen the immune system	Nourish skin and hair, help heal wounds	Aid concentration	Promote happiness
Cabbage	Promotes muscle tone and intestinal health	Contributes to skin radiance, aids in wound healing	Helps get the creative juices flowing	Enhances mood

In

asparagus in spring, bell peppers in summer, pumpkins in fall, red cabbage in winter • roasting and grilling vegetables • snacking on carrots, not candy • organic vegetables • vegetable curries • *always in: strolling around the farmers' market*

Out

Asparagus in winter, etc.— in other words, eating vegetables out of season • always boiling • vegetables with white sauce • using only frozen vegetables • intolerant extreme vegetarians • pureed vegetables • *never, ever in: people who won't eat vegetables—ever*

Family Ties?

No one can choose their family—not even asparagus, King of the Vegetable Patch, can do that. In the kaleidoscopically-colored botanical world there are all sorts of families. But which of those listed below are really brothers and sisters?

a   savoy cabbage and radishes
b   broccoli and arugula
c   lettuce and artichokes
d   potatoes and sweet potatoes
e   spinach and beets
f   onions and asparagus
g   potatoes and tomatoes

Our Favorite Vegetable

The Tomato

French: tomate; Italian: pomodoro; Spanish: tomate

Tomatoes have:
• about 35 calories per medium tomato
• hardly any protein and fat
• similar fiber to a slice of whole-wheat bread
• lots of carotene and vitamin C

Tomatoes can:
• protect you against everyday bugs, like colds
• pump you with energy
• ward off stress
• nourish hair and skin from within

Tomatoes need:
• to be stored at room temperature—never refrigerated (they'll turn mealy)
• to be cut with a serrated knife
• to be seasoned or marinated just 15 minutes before serving
• to be heated gently and briefly

Tomatoes love:
• olive oil, and butter, too!
• black pepper, curry powder, basil, oregano, tarragon, cilantro, onions, and garlic
• a pinch of sugar to bring out their flavor when cooking

Solution: all of them except d

Vegetable Platter with Aïoli

You've gotta like garlic for this one

Feeds 6-8:

For the aïoli (homemade garlic mayo from the south of France):

1 piece white bread without crust (about the size of a medium potato)

2 ½ cups milk

4 medium cloves garlic (more or less to taste)

1 super-fresh egg yolk

3/4 cup good olive oil

Fresh lemon juice

Salt, freshly ground pepper

For the vegetable platter:

1 pound boiling potatoes (unpeeled)

Salt

3-4 eggs

1 pound fresh green beans

2 small bulbs fennel

4 medium carrots

1/2 small head cauliflower (or broccoli)

2-3 tablespoons good olive oil

1 bunch celery

1-2 bell peppers (red, yellow or green)

1 bunch green onions

1 To make the aïoli, first briefly soak the white bread in the milk. Then, squeeze out the milk and put the bread in a bowl. Peel the garlic and squeeze it through a press into the bowl with the bread. Add the yolk and mix the ingredients into a smooth paste. Now add the oil, but not all at once— trickle it into the bowl in a thin stream while beating constantly with a whisk. Season the mixture with lemon juice, salt, and pepper to taste. Chill until ready to use.

2 Wash the potatoes and place in a saucepan. Barely cover them with salted water, bring to a boil, and simmer for 25-35 minutes (depending on size) until they're tender all the way through. Put the eggs in a saucepan of cold water, bring them to a boil, and then reduce the heat to a simmer for 7-8 minutes. Rinse under cold water.

3 Wash the green beans, cut off the ends, and pull off any strings. In a pot, bring 2 quarts of salted water to a boil. Toss in the beans and cook for 8-10 minutes, until they're tender, but still slightly crisp at the center. Pour off the hot water and rinse the beans briefly under cold water.

4 Wash the fennel, cut off any thick stalk portions, and quarter the bulbs or cut into segments. Peel the carrots, quarter them lengthwise, or cut in half. Divide the cauliflower (or broccoli) into small florets, cutting off the stems.

5 In a large nonstick skillet, heat the olive oil over medium heat. Add the fennel, carrots, and cauliflower and sauté for 10-15 minutes. Cover the pan, but stir the vegetables frequently. (Alternately, you can cook all of the vegetables in a little stock in a covered pot until tender.)

6 Wash the celery, and trim both ends. Wash and halve the bell peppers, and remove the stems, ribs, and seeds. Cut the pepper halves into broad strips. Wash the green onions, discard any wilted parts, and cut off the root ends. Leave the onions whole.

7 Drain the boiled potatoes and peel if desired. Crack the eggs, and peel, rinse, and halve lengthwise. Arrange the eggs and vegetables decoratively on serving platters. Fill little bowls with the aioli and put them out on the table so that everyone can reach to dip the vegetables, potatoes, and eggs—that's what the aïoli's there for!

Prep time: 1¼ hours
Good with: crunchy bread, white wine
Calories per serving (8): 510

Tip for Big Bashes:
Precook everything (except the potatoes—do those at the last minute). When ready to serve, lay the vegetables on a baking sheet, cover with foil, and heat in a 350°F oven to warm through.

Artichokes with Vinaigrette
A really easy party dish

Feeds 4 as an appetizer:

4 large artichokes

Salt

1-2 tablespoons Dijon-style mustard

4-5 tablespoons white wine vinegar (or fresh lemon juice)

7-8 tablespoons olive oil or vegetable oil

Freshly ground pepper

2 sprigs fresh dill (or 1 bunch fresh chives)

1 Wash the artichokes, and cut off the stalks close to the artichoke bases. Using kitchen scissors or a very sharp knife, cut off the top third of the leaf tips.

2 Place the artichokes in a pot so that they're sitting next to one another, and pour in enough water to cover the lower half of the artichokes. Add a touch of salt, cover the pot, and bring to a boil over high heat. Turn down the heat to medium, and simmer the artichokes for 30-40 minutes, depending on size. Pull off one of the outer leaves from time to time to see if they're done—as soon as a leaf comes away easily, the artichokes are probably ready. Turn an artichoke upside down and stick a paring knife into the bottom to be sure—it should be very tender.

3 While the artichokes are cooking, make the vinaigrette for dipping: Whisk together the mustard and white wine vinegar (or lemon juice). Then, blend in the oil. Season with salt and pepper to taste. Wash the dill (or chives), shake dry, very finely chop, and stir into the vinaigrette.

4 Remove the artichokes from the pot, turn them upside down to drain, and set on serving plates. Divide the vinaigrette among 4 little bowls. To eat, pull the leaves one by one from the artichoke, dip the fleshy end in the vinaigrette, and draw it between your teeth to scrape off the tender flesh.

5 When all of the outside leaves have been chewed on, you'll get to the part you can't eat: the hairy, prickly "choke"—you can remove it with a knife or small spoon to expose the artichoke heart underneath. The heart is the tastiest part—make sure you have plenty of vinaigrette left for this delicate morsel.

137

Prep time: 45 minutes
Good with: crunchy bread
Calories per serving: 185

Assortment of Asparagus
A must in May!

White asparagus can be hard to find in this country, but it's really popular in Europe. Browse through the stands at the weekend farmers' market or specialty food store in the early spring, when asparagus is in season. If you can't find white asparagus, double the recipe for the vinaigrette-dressed green asparagus; accompany it with the potatoes, tossed with the melted butter and chopped fresh parsley.

Feeds 4-6:

2¼ pounds white asparagus

Salt

Pinch of sugar

1 tablespoon butter + 1/2 cup butter to melt

2 pounds green asparagus

2 pounds small boiling potatoes

4 tablespoons balsamic vinegar

Freshly ground pepper

6 tablespoons olive oil

1 tablespoon capers (drained)

A few fresh basil leaves

Grated lemon zest

Chopped fresh Italian parsley

1 Carefully peel the white asparagus: You need a vegetable peeler that's not too blunt or beaten up—otherwise it's a bit of a drag. Set your nice sharp peeler blade just below the head of one asparagus spear and pull downwards. Rotate the spear several times and repeat to peel completely. Cut off the lower woody part of the spear (you'll feel this as you peel). Don't hesitate to cut—if you don't cut off enough you'll get nasty strings between your teeth as you eat and it'll spoil your asparagus experience!

2 Boil the white asparagus: put the stalks in a wide saucepan and cover with water. Add a sprinkling of salt, the sugar, and 1 tablespoon butter. Cover the pan and bring to a boil; reduce the heat to medium and cook for 15-20 minutes, until the stalks are tender.

3 Peel the green asparagus—again, you want a really sharp peeler to strip off just the lower third of the stalk. Cut off the bottom woody portion of each spear.

4 Boil the green asparagus: put the spears in a wide saucepan and cover with water. Add a sprinkling of salt and bring to a boil. Cover the pan, reduce the heat to medium, and cook for 8-10 minutes, until tender, but still slightly crisp in the center.

5 Wash the potatoes, place in a saucepan, just barely cover with salted water, and simmer until tender (about 20 minutes). Melt the 1/2 cup butter in a small saucepan and keep warm.

6 Drain the green asparagus and place it in a serving dish. In a small bowl, mix the balsamic vinegar, salt and pepper to taste, and the olive oil, and drizzle it over the warm asparagus. Scatter the capers, basil leaves, and lemon zest to taste over the top.

7 Drain the white asparagus and place it on a preheated serving dish. Serve with the boiled potatoes, parsley, and hot butter.

Prep time: 1½ hours
Calories per serving (6): 345

Basic Tips

Traditional accompaniments to white asparagus are sliced cooked ham or salmon steaks. It also tastes great rolled inside thin pancakes with hollandaise sauce (see pages 52 and 98).

Green asparagus is wonderful roasted instead of boiled. After trimming and peeling, cut the spears into segments. Toss the segments in a roasting pan with a touch of olive oil or butter. Roast in a 450°F oven until tender-crisp (about 20 minutes). Season with salt and freshly ground pepper. Then, drizzle with a little lemon juice and scatter chopped herbs or freshly grated Parmesan over the top.

Veggie Gratin
With 1001 variations

Feeds 4:

2 pounds butternut squash

1¼ pounds boiling potatoes

1 bunch green onions

2 red bell peppers

2 tablespoons butter

1¼ cups milk

1 cup heavy cream

1 egg (lightly beaten)

5 tablespoons grated Swiss cheese

1 teaspoon dried thyme

Freshly ground nutmeg

Salt, freshly ground pepper

1 Peel the squash and potatoes and cut them into thin slices. Wash the green onions, and chop off any wilted parts and the root ends. Halve the onions lengthwise, and cut into 1½- to 2-inch pieces. Halve the bell peppers lengthwise, and remove the stems, ribs, and seeds. Rinse the peppers, and cut into fine strips.

2 Preheat the oven to 350°F. Grease a large ovenproof dish with some of the butter. In a bowl, mix the milk, cream, and egg. Mix in the cheese, thyme, nutmeg, salt, and lots of pepper to taste.

3 Layer the squash, potatoes, and green onions in the dish, and scatter the pepper strips on top. Pour the egg-milk mixture over the top and dot with the rest of the butter. Bake for about 1 hour on the middle oven shelf, until the vegetables are tender. After 40 minutes (or sooner: keep checking the progress by peeking through the window in the oven's door), cover the dish with foil so that the top doesn't get too dark.

Prep time: busy 30 minutes, relaxing 1 hour
Good with: crunchy bread
Calories per serving: 580

Tip
Making gratins is really easy: Wash and trim any combination of vegetables, and chop them up small. First throw any dense vegetables (like carrots, celery, cauliflower, and green beans) into boiling salted water until partially cooked, then rinse and drain. Then, layer them in a greased dish with any other not-so-dense vegetables (like zucchini, eggplant, potatoes, and squash). Pour over the egg-milk mixture and bake. You can jazz things up with ham, smoked chicken or turkey, cheese, or herbs.

Stuffed Peppers
An old-fashioned treat

Feeds 4:

1/2 cup rice

1 cup water

Salt

1/2 bunch fresh Italian parsley

1 onion

2 cloves garlic

2 tablespoons vegetable oil

1 large can peeled tomatoes (28 ounces)

Freshly ground pepper

10 ounces ground meat (beef, turkey, pork)

1 egg

1 tablespoon hot mustard

Cayenne pepper

1 teaspoon dried oregano

4 same-sized large green bell peppers

1 Add the rice and water to a saucepan. Add a touch of salt, cover, and bring just to a boil. Simmer over medium heat for about 10 minutes, then pour off the water, drain well, and set aside to cool.

2 Wash the parsley, shake dry, and finely chop. Peel and chop the onion and garlic.

3 In a large, deep saucepan, sauté half of the chopped onion in the oil over medium heat until it's translucent. Add the tomatoes with their juice, and break them up into small pieces. Season with salt and pepper to taste, cover, and simmer over low heat, stirring occasionally.

4 Use your hands (make sure they're clean!) to mix the ground meat with rest of the onion, the garlic, parsley, egg, and mustard. Mix in the cooled rice, too. Season well with salt, pepper, and cayenne pepper to taste, and the oregano.

5 Wash the peppers and slice off the tops, leaving the stem intact. Cut out the ribs, and wash out the seeds. Fill the peppers with the meat stuffing, dividing evenly, and set the pepper tops back on.

6 Place the stuffed peppers in the pan with the tomato sauce, cover the pan, and cook over medium-low heat for 45 minutes, until the peppers are tender.

Prep time: busy 30 minutes, baking
45 minutes
Calories per serving: 510

Variation: Baked Stuffed Tomatoes

Wash and dry 8 large tomatoes, and slice the top off each one. Spoon out the seeds and discard. With the spoon, hollow out the tomato cavities, reserving the flesh. Chop the flesh and put it in a small bowl. Turn the hollowed-out tomatoes upside down in a colander to drain. Remove the crust from 4 medium slices of white sandwich bread, and cut the bread into cubes. Fry the bread cubes in 2 tablespoons olive oil, and push 2 cloves of garlic through a press into the pan. Preheat the oven to 400°F. Shred 8 ounces of Romano cheese, mix it in a bowl with 2-3 tablespoons crème fraîche, and season it with salt and pepper to taste. Add a tablespoon or so of finely chopped fresh thyme or Italian parsley, 1 tablespoon capers (drained), and the toasted bread cubes; mix well. Divide the filling among the tomatoes, set the tops back on, and stand the tomatoes in a lightly oiled ovenproof dish. Pour the reserved chopped tomato flesh and juice over and around the stuffed tomatoes, season everything with salt and pepper, and drizzle with 3 tablespoons olive oil. Bake for about 20 minutes. Goes well with green salad.

Stir-Fried Vegetables
Change the vegetables to suit your mood

Feeds 4:

1/2 ounce dried mushrooms

1 large leek

2 large carrots

1 large red bell pepper

1 can bamboo shoots (8 ounces)

2-4 cloves garlic

1 piece fresh ginger (thumb sized)

4-5 tablespoons soy sauce

2 tablespoons sake (rice wine)

3-4 tablespoons vegetable oil

1/4-3/4 teaspoon red chile flakes

Salt, freshly ground pepper

4 ounces bean sprouts

1 The most important thing to remember when you're about to use a wok (apart from the wok itself) is that you have a really large cutting board and a really sharp knife on hand. Otherwise, the whole chopping routine will be a drag—and chopping is what this recipe is all about. It's also a good idea to get out a couple of little dishes, so that the vegetables can go right into them after being chopped.

2 Before you start cutting, soften the dried mushrooms: put them in a small bowl and cover with boiling water.

3 Now let's chop! Clean the leek—in other words, cut off the root end and everything green that's floppy, tough, and/or wilted. Then, slit the leek lengthwise and wash it well under running water, especially between the inside layers. Cut the leek crosswise into very fine slices.

4 Peel the carrots and cut them into thin lengthwise slices; then, cut the slices into matchstick strips. Wash the bell pepper, halve lengthwise, and cut out the stem, ribs,

and seeds. Cut the pepper halves into matchstick strips. Drain the bamboo shoots and cut them into matchstick strips. Place all of the vegetables into separate dishes.

5 The mushrooms are probably soft by now—strain them through a coffee filter, setting the soaking liquid aside for later. Rinse the mushrooms briefly, drain them, chop off the stems, and cut them up small.

6 Peel and mince the garlic and ginger, and place in separate bowls. In a small bowl, stir together the soy sauce and sake. Set the wok on the stove over high heat and make sure all your ingredients are at arm's length.

7 Pour the oil into the hot wok. Toss in the garlic, ginger, and chile flakes, and stir-fry for a few seconds. Next, throw in a handful of leeks, and stir-fry. Throw in the rest of the leeks, and stir-fry some more. Now, move what's already cooked to edge of the wok to make room for more raw vegetables. This time, add a portion of carrot sticks to the middle of the wok and stir-fry. Then, toss in the rest of the carrots, the mushrooms, bell peppers, bamboo shoots—the chef can decide in which order. Usually you'd begin with the tougher vegetables and lightly stir-fry the more delicate ones at the end—but you know, it's really just a matter of taste. Since everything is so finely chopped anyway, you'll only need 5 minutes max for the whole stir-fry event.

8 Pour the soy sauce-sake mixture into the wok, then mix in a couple of small spoonfuls of the reserved mushroom soaking liquid, and maybe a shot of water. Season with salt and pepper to taste, and simmer for about a minute. Right at the end, add the sprouts, and stir-fry briefly just to warm them. Taste the vegetables and get them out of pan before they overcook. Hide the knives and forks—get out the chopsticks!

Prep time: 45 minutes
Good with: rice, of course!
Calories per serving: 180

Curried Potatoes and Mushrooms
Paste makes perfect!

Feeds 4:

1½ pounds small boiling potatoes

Salt

Generous 1 pound fresh oyster mushrooms (or small white mushrooms)

2-3 cloves garlic

Freshly ground pepper

1/4 cup olive oil

2 tablespoons fresh lemon juice

3 stalks celery

1 bunch green onions

A couple of mild red chiles, fresh or marinated

1/2 bunch fresh Italian parsley

1 tablespoon curry paste (look for it in jars in the Asian section of the market—there are lots of different kinds, from mild to hot)

1 Scrub the potatoes under running water with a vegetable brush. Put the potatoes in a pot and barely cover with water. Add a smidgen of salt, cover the pot, and bring to a boil over high heat. Then, turn down the heat and simmer the potatoes for about 15-20 minutes, until they're soft.

2 While the potatoes are doing their thing, you have a quiet moment to clean the mushrooms—it's better to wipe them clean rather than wash them, otherwise they quickly soak up lots of water. Cut off the thick, hard mushroom "feet." Chop the mushroom caps a little smaller. Peel and mince the garlic. Put the mushrooms in a bowl with the garlic, a touch of salt and pepper, 2 tablespoons of the olive oil, and the lemon juice.

3 Wash the celery, and cut off the parts at the ends that no longer look crunchy and fresh. Cut the stalks into very thin slices. Clean and wash the green onions: remove the root ends and wilted green parts. Then, cut the onions diagonally into thin slices. Wash the fresh chiles, or drain the marinated ones, and cut into smaller pieces.

4 Once the potatoes are soft, pour off the water and let them sit for a while to drive off the steam. Peel the potatoes with a paring knife while still hot, and halve or quarter them. Wash the parsley, shake dry, and coarsely chop.

5 Heat a wok or large skillet over medium-high heat, pour in the remaining 2 tablespoons oil, and wait a second or two until it's hot enough to sizzle. Add the celery and green onions, and stir-fry for 1 minute. Push the vegetables to one side of the pan, then add the mushrooms and their marinade to the center of the pan. Stir-fry for a few moments. Scatter the chiles over the top.

6 Add the potatoes and mix them well with everything else. Stir in the curry paste and stir-fry everything together for another 1-2 minutes. Season with salt and pepper to taste and sprinkle the parsley over the top.

Prep time: 50 minutes
Calories per serving: 240

Braised Spring Vegetables
Veggies for a good mood

Feeds 4:

10 ounces broccoli

3 stalks celery

1/2 pound asparagus

1/2 pound snow peas

1 bunch green onions

Generous 1 pound small tomatoes

Salt

Juice from 1 lemon

2 tablespoons butter

Freshly ground pepper and nutmeg

2 tablespoons balsamic vinegar

Leaves from 1 bunch small-leafed fresh basil

2 tablespoons freshly grated Parmesan cheese

1 Wash all of the vegetables. Cut the broccoli into small florets. Peel the tender broccoli stalks and cut into slices; discard any woody broccoli stalks.

2 Cut off any bits off celery that don't look fresh any more, and cut the stalks into chunks. Cut the woody ends off the asparagus spears and chop them just like the celery.

3 Cut off the ends off the snow peas and pull off the strings. Cut away the root ends and any wilted green parts from the green onions. Cut off all but about 1½ inches of the green onions; chop the rest of the green parts into tiny rings. Briefly plunge the tomatoes into boiling water, rinse in cold water, remove the skins with a paring knife, and cut into eighths.

4 In a big pot, bring 2-3 quarts of salted water to a boil, and add the lemon juice. Add the asparagus, then, at 1 minute intervals, throw in the celery, broccoli florets, and snow peas. Boil the veggies for another 2 minutes. Drain, saving the broth. Rinse the vegetables under cold running water and drain well.

5 Put a deep-sided skillet on the stovetop over medium heat. Melt the butter in the pan, add the white parts of the green onions and the broccoli stems, and sauté them in the butter for 2-3 minutes. Then, add the drained vegetables, pour in a couple spoonfuls of the vegetable cooking broth, and stir in the tomato pieces.

6 Braise the vegetables for another 10 minutes and season with salt, pepper, and nutmeg to taste, and the balsamic vinegar. Scatter the green onion rings, basil leaves, and Parmesan over the top.

Prep time: 50 minutes
Calories per serving: 155

Ratatouille
The essence of summer

Feeds 4:

2¼ pounds ripe tomatoes

1 pound eggplant

1 pound zucchini

1 red, 1 green, and 1 yellow bell pepper

2 fresh or marinated chiles

2 medium onions

3-4 cloves garlic

Olive oil

Salt, freshly ground pepper

1 sprig fresh rosemary

1 Plunge the tomatoes in boiling water for about a minute. Rinse them under cold water, then remove the skins with a paring knife. Cut the tomatoes in half, scrape out the seeds, and coarsely chop.

2 Wash the eggplant and cut into 1/4-1/2-inch cubes. Place the cubes in a colander, sprinkle well with salt, and let them stand for a while over a sink. Wash the zucchini, and cut it into thin slices—if the zucchini are large, cut the slices in half. Wash the peppers, cut them in half, and remove the stems, ribs, and seeds. Cut the peppers into pieces about the same size as the eggplant.

144

3 Slit open the chiles, and remove the stems and seeds. Chop them into small pieces. Peel the onions, cut them in half, and then into slices. Peel and mince the garlic. Wash the salt off the diced eggplant, drain well, and pat dry with paper towels.

4 In a large pot, heat 3-4 tablespoons olive oil over medium heat. Add the onion and garlic and sauté until translucent. Then, add the vegetables one by one and stir-fry: chunks of bell pepper first, then the eggplant, zucchini, and chiles. Keep adding oil as you need more.

5 Season the vegetables with salt and pepper to taste. The last thing: add the tomatoes and rosemary, cover the pan, and cook for about 45 minutes, until the vegetables are tender (stir occasionally). Before serving, remove the rosemary, and season again with salt and pepper to taste.

Prep time: 1½ hours
Calories per serving: 250

Eggplant Parmesan
A retro basic

Feeds 4:

1 eggplant (about 1 pound)

All-purpose flour

2 eggs, lightly beaten

3/4 cup dry bread crumbs, seasoned with

salt and freshly ground pepper

Vegetable oil for frying

6 ounces mozzarella cheese

1 ounce Parmesan cheese, freshly grated

1 cup of your favorite spaghetti sauce

1 Wash the eggplant and cut it into thin slices.

2 Place the flour, eggs, and bread crumbs in separate shallow bowls. Dredge the eggplant slices in flour, followed by eggs, followed by bread crumbs; remember to shake off the excess after each step.

3 Heat about 1/4 inch of oil in a high-sided skillet until very hot, but not smoking. Add the eggplant slices and fry until golden brown on both sides. Carefully transfer the cooked eggplant slices to paper towels.

4 Heat the broiler. Cut the cheese into thin slices. Place the eggplant slices on a foil-lined baking sheet and spread with a little bit of tomato sauce. Top each slice with a slice of mozzarella, and sprinkle with the Parmesan cheese. Place the pan under the broiler and cook until the cheese is melted and lightly browned.

5 Pour the remaining tomato sauce into a saucepan and heat through.

6 To serve, divide the tomato sauce among the serving plates and top with the eggplant rounds.

Prep time: 45 minutes
Cool idea: spread the eggplant slices with pesto (see p 89) instead of tomato sauce
Good with: red wine, green salad, good crusty bread
Calories per serving: 370

Glazed Carrots
Simply scrumptious

Feeds 4 as a side dish:

1 pound carrots

Salt

1/4 cup butter

1 teaspoon sugar

2-3 sprigs fresh Italian parsley

Fresh basil, mint, or chives

1 Peel the carrots, and trim off the tops. Halve or quarter the carrots if they are very thick. Chop them into 1-inch pieces.

2 Put the carrots in a skillet in a single layer, barely cover them with water, and sprinkle them lightly with salt. Simmer the carrots over medium heat for 5-10 minutes, until they're softened, but still crunchy. Now, carefully pour out the liquid until just 1-2 tablespoons is left in pan.

3 Add pats of the butter to the pan and sprinkle with the sugar. Sauté the carrots for another 5 minutes over low heat, stirring constantly so they glaze evenly. Sprinkle with the herbs, freshly chopped to taste.

Prep time: 25 minutes
Good with: meat, poultry, fish
Calories per serving: 130

Spicy Broccoli
Piquant side dish

Feeds 4:

1 head broccoli

1 tablespoon chicken stock (or water)

1 tablespoon soy sauce

1 tablespoon rice vinegar (or white vinegar)

2 teaspoons cornstarch

1 tablespoon vegetable oil

1/4 teaspoon toasted sesame oil

1/8-1/4 teaspoon red chile flakes

1 Wash the broccoli. Cut the broccoli into small florets. In a small bowl, combine the stock (or water), soy sauce, vinegar, and cornstarch. Set aside.

2 Get a wok or large skillet hot, then add the vegetable oil and sesame oil. Stir in the chile flakes briefly. Add the broccoli and stir-fry for 3-4 minutes, until tender when you first bite into it, but still slightly crisp at the center.

3 Stir the soy sauce mixture and pour it into the pan. Stir-fry just until the broccoli is coated with the thickened sauce.

Prep time: 20 minutes
Good with: rice, other stir-fried dishes, Chinese beer
Calories per serving: 75

Sautéed Zucchini
Mediterranean 101

Feeds 4 as a side dish:

Generous 1 pound zucchini

2 cloves garlic

3 tablespoons olive oil

Salt, freshly ground pepper

1 tablespoon fresh lemon juice

1 tablespoon balsamic vinegar

1 Wash the zucchini and cut into slices. Halve the slices if they're large. Or, cut the zucchini into sticks.

2 Peel and mince the garlic. In a skillet, heat the olive oil over medium heat. Add the zucchini and sauté for a minute or two. Then, add the garlic and sauté for 5 more minutes, until the zucchini is tender. Season with salt and pepper to taste, and drizzle with the lemon juice and balsamic vinegar.

Prep time: 20 minutes
Good with: grilled stuff, lamb
Calories per serving: 70

Tip:
This recipe also tastes good mixed with 1 teaspoon of ready-made pesto just before serving.

Prep time: 15 minutes, plus cooking time
Good with: poultry, spinach
Calories per serving: 260

Sesame Spinach
Makes you strong

Feeds 4 as a side dish:

2¼ pounds fresh spinach

3 tablespoons sesame seeds

2 tablespoons olive oil

Salt, freshly ground pepper

2 tablespoons fresh lemon juice

1 Wash the spinach by swishing it vigorously in a sinkful of water. Snap off the thick stems, and put the leaves in a colander.

2 Set a really big skillet on the stove and turn the heat to high. Toss in the wet spinach and cover the pan. After a few minutes, the spinach leaves will be wilted—now you'll see why you schlepped mountains of it home with you: there's not really very much left.

3 Let the spinach cool a little, press out the excess liquid, and coarsely chop. Place the skillet back on the stove, wipe it out, and heat over medium heat. Add the sesame seeds and briefly toast them in the pan. Then, pour in the oil. Add the chopped spinach and stir well, then season with salt and pepper to taste, and the lemon juice.

Prep time: 35 minutes
Good with: meat, poultry
Calories per serving: 105

Savory Lentils
Better than baked beans

Feeds 4 as a side dish:

1 cup lentils

1 bay leaf

1 small sweet onion

5 tablespoons olive oil

1/2 cup dry white wine

3 tablespoons white wine vinegar

1 teaspoon hot mustard

Salt, freshly ground pepper

2 tablespoons chopped fresh chives

1 Put the lentils and bay leaf in a saucepan and cover with cold water. Cover the pan and cook over medium heat till the lentils are soft, but still slightly firm (40-60 minutes).

2 Peel the onions and finely slice. Sauté in 2 tablespoons of the oil over medium-low heat until translucent. Pour in the wine and simmer for a few minutes. Remove from the heat.

3 Drain the lentils. Mix the warm lentils well with the sautéed onion. In a small bowl, blend the vinegar with the remaining 3 tablespoons oil and the mustard, pour over the lentils, and stir well. Season generously with salt and pepper to taste. Sprinkle the chives over the top.

Snow Peas with Lemon Butter
Fast and good

Feeds 4 as a side dish:

Generous 1 pound snow peas

2 tablespoons butter

Zest from 1 lemon, and 1-2 tablespoons of the lemon juice

Salt, freshly ground pepper

Pinch of sugar

1 Wash the snow peas, drain, cut off the pointy ends, and pull off any strings.

2 In a skillet, melt the butter and stir in half of the lemon zest. Add the snow peas, toss them in the lemon butter, and sauté for 8-10 minutes. The peas should be tender when you first bite into them, but be still nice and crisp in the center. Season with salt and pepper to taste, the lemon juice, and sugar. Sprinkle with the remaining lemon zest before serving.

147

Prep time: 20 minutes
Good with: fish, poultry
Calories per serving: 100

Sweet

How do you like your sweets? Fruity...fancy....or warm and cuddly?

S

How Sweet Are You?
Take the test to find out!

1. The person you've had a crush on treats you to dinner.
What do you drink?
a. Herbal tea
b. Espresso milkshake
c. Fresh-squeezed orange juice

2. Now your crush is making dinner for you. When the dessert is just about to arrive you remember that you have to be somewhere else. What do you do?
a. Stay, of course
b. Go, what else?
c. Depends on dessert

3. Now it's the first breakfast at the crush's place. What'll make you happy now?
a. French toast with homemade fruit butter
b. Granola with yogurt and fruit
c. Nutella (chocolate-hazelnut spread) and a spoon

Solution: see page 151

Five Five-Minute Sweet Sauces

Speedy Fruit Sauce
Puree canned fruit, such as peaches, apricots, or pineapple, with a little bit of their juice; add fresh lemon juice and/or your favorite liqueur to taste (you can also use fresh or frozen fruit instead of canned fruit and sweeten it with confectioner's sugar). Tastes good with anything that goes with fruit.

Speedy Cherry Sauce
1 Pour a large bottle or can of sweet or sour cherries (do not use maraschino) into a colander and save the juice.
2 Mix 4 tablespoons of the juice with 2 tablespoons of vanilla pudding powder and 2 tablespoons sugar. Bring the rest of the juice to a boil, remove the pan from the heat, stir in the vanilla-cherry mixture, and bring back to a boil.
3 Stir in the drained cherries and let cool. Tastes good with pastries or ice cream.

Speedy Vanilla Sauce
1 Prepare one package of "Cook & Serve" vanilla pudding as described on the package, but use 1½ times the amount of milk called for.
2 Vanilla sauce is good with baked desserts, such as bread pudding, fruit desserts, chocolate, and cakes. A bonus: stir in a dash of cocoa powder, and presto–you've got chocolate sauce.

Speedy Chocolate Sauce
1 Heat 1/2 cup of heavy cream and 4 oz of your favorite chocolate, broken into pieces. Stir until smooth.
2 Depending on your mood, add brandy, fruit schnapps, liqueur, rum, or instant coffee granules to taste. Tastes good with creamy desserts, chocolate-loving fruits, and pastries.

Speedy Mascarpone Sauce
1 Squeeze the juice from 1 orange and blend with an 8-oz tub of mascarpone cheese (rich Italian cream cheese), 1 tablespoon honey, and a shot of amaretto. Tastes good with fruit salad, chocolate ice cream, waffles, and pancakes.

In
strawberries in spring, melon in summer, grapes in fall, papaya in winter • knowing more than three varieties of apples • occasionally using honey or syrup instead of sugar • desserts made with coconut milk • old classics • variations on a theme, such as chocolate crème brulée, white chocolate bread pudding, raspberry shortcake • making whipped cream by hand • *Always fashionable: vanilla pudding or custard, ice cream, and anything chocolate*

Out
strawberries at Christmas, grapes at Easter, oranges in summer, rhubarb in fall • thinking that all apples are the same • all sugar, no taste • believing that the dish should look good, whatever the cost • dessert platters with uncomplimentary elements • a sweet dish that fills you up all by itself • *Never, ever in style: no dessert at all*

How Sweet are you?

Solution to test on Page 149

1a: 1 point 1b: 3 points 1c: 2 points
2a: 3 points 2b: 0 points 2c: 1 point
3a: 2 points 3b: 0 points 3c: 3 points

7-9 points: you're quite a sweetie!

For you, dessert has to be something cuddly, in other words soft and preferably still warm, so you can lounge happily on the couch. That's OK—but remember, in the long run, there are better things for cuddling.

Your sweet dishes: crème caramel, chocolate pudding, fried batter with mascarpone, baked apples, bread pudding, and Nona's sweet polenta pudding: Bring 2 cups of milk to a boil, pour in 1/3 cup of instant polenta or grits, and boil for 5 minutes, stirring constantly. In a bowl, beat 1 egg white together with 1 pinch salt and 1 tablespoon sugar until stiff; beat 1 yolk quickly into the cooked polenta. Fold in the whipped egg white.

4-6 points: You've got a sweet tooth, but it's an elegant one.

Just sweet is too simple for you. What you really want is a sophisticated surprise for dessert. That's a challenge—and a source of frustration. So we're going to ask you to tone it down a bit: homey chocolate pudding can be just as satisfying as chocolate mousse.

Your sweet dishes: panna cotta, orange mousse, crêpes Suzette, lemon tart, chocolate mousse, and *Caffe alla Pappa*: slip one scoop of vanilla ice cream into a glass, pour over 1 cup of strong hot espresso and 1 shot brandy, sprinkle with chopped chocolate-covered coffee beans, and serve immediately—simple sophistication.

1-3 points:You think sweets are quite nice—only if they are healthy, bright, and effortless.

That's why you'd rather sink your teeth into a sour apple than keep having to check the oven.

Your sweet dishes: homemade "Jell-O", fruit salad (gratinée, if it has to come that way) and blueberry muffins, and apple ricotta: blend 8 ounces low-fat ricotta cheese with 5 tablespoons organic applesauce, 1 tablespoon honey, and 1 pinch cinnamon, and serve with a couple of Italian almond cookies—quick to make, both refreshing and calming.

Our Favorite Fruit

The Apple

French: pomme; Italian: mela;
Spanish: manzana

Apples are:
• Europe's most popular fruit, and the third most popular fruit worldwide (after citrus fruits and bananas)
  • available year 'round all the way down to New Zealand
  • diverse in name and variety: e.g. Braeburn, Fuji, Granny Smith, Jonathan, Lady, McIntosh, Pippin, Red or Golden Delicious, Winesap

Apples have:
• about 80 calories per medium apple
• 22 g carbohydrates
• hardly any fat or protein
• lots of fiber and pectin
• a decent amount of vitamin C

Apples can:
• stimulate digestion
• contribute to breath freshness and vitality
• keep the doctor away (one a day)

Apples want:
• to be treated gently—they bruise easily
• to be stored in a cool, dry place, but NOT in the refrigerator
• to be stored away from potatoes or lemons, which make them spoil faster
• to be used quickly once peeled, or they turn brown
• to be cooked gently and rapidly

Apples love:
• butter, cream, cheese
• anise seeds, vanilla, cinnamon, sugar
• almonds, walnuts, raisins, lemon
• curry, horseradish, pepper, salt

Panna Cotta with Berry Compote

Sinfully Rich!

Using all cream instead of part milk makes this an even bigger vice!

Feeds 8:

1¾ cup heavy cream

2½ cups milk (or heavy cream)

5 tablespoons + 1/4 cup sugar

Pinch of salt

2 vanilla beans

2 envelopes unflavored gelatin

1 pound mixed berries (strawberries, raspberries, blackberries—whatever is fresh and cheap)

1 Pour the cream and 2 cups of the milk (or cream) into a saucepan and stir in 5 tablespoons sugar, and the salt. With a small sharp knife, slit the vanilla beans lengthwise, and with the tip of the knife, scrape out the vanilla seeds and stir them into the cream-milk mixture (this will make little black dots in the cream). Throw the empty vanilla beans in the pot, too.

2 Heat the contents of the pan over low heat and simmer gently for 15 minutes, stirring occasionally. Place the remaining 1/2 cup milk (or cream) in a cup, sprinkle it with the gelatin, and let stand for a few minutes, until softened, then stir to blend.

3 Remove from the heat, and stir in the gelatin mixture, until dissolved. Fish out the vanilla beans, and let the mixture cool a little.

4 Stir the creamy mixture, then pour it into 8 small metal molds or porcelain soufflé dishes (about 3/4 cup capacity), which have been rinsed with cold water. Cool to room temperature, and refrigerate overnight.

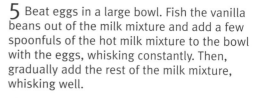

5 Rinse and drain the berries . Discard the stems, leaves, and any bruised parts. Cut the strawberries, if using, into small pieces. In a saucepan, warm the berries with the 1/4 cup sugar, and cook lightly, until the berries just start to soften.

6 To release the *panna cottas* from the molds, warm a thin knife under hot water and run the tip around the insides of each mold. Or, submerge the bottom of each mold briefly in hot water. Invert the panna cottas onto serving plates and spoon the berry compote over the top and around the sides.

Prep time: 40 minutes
Good with: espresso—before, during, or after
Calories per serving: 290

Crème Caramel
Everyone loves it

Feeds 6:

1/2 cup sugar

2 tablespoons water

2 cups milk (or heavy cream)

Pinch of salt

1 vanilla bean

4 eggs

1 First, prepare the caramel syrup: in a little saucepan, bring 1/4 cup of the sugar and the water to a boil over low heat, stirring continuously. Allow the syrup to brown very lightly, then quickly remove it from the heat.

2 Divide the syrup among 6 little ovenproof dishes or ramekins (each big enough to hold 1/2-3/4 cup), and tilt the dishes so that the syrup evenly covers the bottom of each one.

3 Preheat the oven to 350°F. Fill a deep-sided baking pan 1/4 full with water, and set it on the lowest shelf of the oven.

4 Put the milk, (or cream) salt, and remaining 1/4 cup sugar in a medium saucepan and heat slowly. With a small, sharp knife, slit the vanilla bean lengthwise, scrape out the seeds, and drop into the milk together with the empty vanilla bean. Turn up the heat and bring the mixture to a boil briefly, then immediately remove the pan from the heat.

5 Beat eggs in a large bowl. Fish the vanilla beans out of the milk mixture and add a few spoonfuls of the hot milk mixture to the bowl with the eggs, whisking constantly. Then, gradually add the rest of the milk mixture, whisking well.

6 Divide the egg-milk mixture among the caramel-coated dishes. Carefully place the dishes in the pan with the water bath and bake for about 20 minutes, until the custard is set. Remove the dishes from the water bath, cool for a while, then refrigerate until chilled (preferably overnight).

7 To serve, briefly submerge the bottom part of the dishes in hot water. Heat a thin knife under hot water and run the tip around the edges of the custard to detach them. Invert the crème caramels onto serving plates, letting the caramel run onto the plates as a sauce.

Prep time: busy 30 minutes, relaxing 20 minutes (plus chilling time)
Good with: espresso
Calories per serving: 190

Variation: Crème Brûlée
In this case the caramel isn't sitting on the bottom, but makes a crispy layer on top of the creamy dessert. Combine the ingredients for the custard (the cream or milk, 1/4 cup sugar, salt, vanilla, and beaten eggs) as described above. Pour the mixture into the dishes and ramekins (without any caramel) and bake them in the hot water bath as directed. Cool and refrigerate. Before serving, put the molds into an ice cold water bath (fill a deep-sided baking pan 1/4 full with cold water and ice cubes). Sprinkle each serving with 1 tablespoon sugar and place the custards briefly under a broiler until a brown crust forms. Let cool once more (to prevent burned lips!) and serve.

Chocolate Pudding
Tastes just like you remember it

Use really good chocolate here, as it will affect the outcome of your pudding.

Feeds 4:

4 ounces semisweet chocolate

2 egg yolks

1/4 cup sugar

2 cups milk

3 tablespoons cornstarch

1 vanilla bean

1 Break or coarsely chop the chocolate into small pieces. Put the egg yolks and sugar in a small bowl and, using a whisk, beat for a few minutes until mixture is nice and creamy.

2 Stir 1/2 cup of the milk together with the cornstarch and pour the remaining 1½ cups of the milk into a saucepan. Add the chocolate to the pan. With a small sharp knife, slit the vanilla bean lengthwise, scrape out the seeds, and add them to the saucepan along with the empty vanilla bean. Bring the chocolate-milk mixture to a boil over medium heat, stirring constantly.

3 Pour the cornstarch–milk mixture into the pan, and simmer over medium heat, stirring, until the mixture thickens. Remove the vanilla bean. Mix in the egg yolk-sugar mixture, but that's it for the heat–the hot pudding mixture will gently cook the eggs.

4 Remove the pan from the heat, stir just a little more, and let the mixture cool slightly. Stir occasionally to prevent a "skin" from forming on the surface.

5 Now, rinse 4 small molds or one 1-quart mold with cold water. Fill the mold(s) with the pudding and chill well in the refrigerator (at least 1-2 hours).

6 To serve, briefly submerge the bottom part of the mold(s) in hot water. Heat a thin knife under hot water and run the tip around the edges of the puddings to detach them. Invert the puddings onto serving plates.

Prep time: 45 minutes, plus chilling time
Good with: vanilla sauce or sweetened whipped cream
Calories per serving: 340

Basic Tip
Vanilla Sauce:

In a saucepan, blend 2 cups milk with 1 teaspoon cornstarch, and the seeds scraped from 1 vanilla bean. In a small bowl, whip 2 egg yolks (or 1 whole egg) with 3 tablespoons sugar, then stir the egg mixture into the milk mixture. At this point apply heat and, stirring all the time, bring the mixture almost—but really only almost—to a boil, until it coats the back of the stirring spoon. Tastes great warm or cold—and not just with chocolate pudding!!

Homemade "Jell-O"
Great for warm-weather dining

Feeds 4-6

1 pint strawberries

1 half-pint raspberries

3/4 cup dried cranberries

1 cup cherry juice

1 tablespoon sugar

1 stick cinnamon

1 cup cranberry juice cocktail

2 envelopes unflavored gelatin

1 Wash the strawberries and remove the stems and cores (hulls). Cut the large berries into halves or quarters to make bite-sized pieces. Sort through the raspberries and toss out the bad ones.

2 In a medium saucepan, combine the dried cranberries, cherry juice, sugar, and cinnamon. Bring to a boil over medium-high heat. Then, turn down the heat to low and simmer for 3 minutes.

3 Pour the cranberry juice into a small bowl. Sprinkle the gelatin over the juice and let stand for about 5 minutes to soften. Stir the gelatin mixture briefly, and add it to the juice mixture in saucepan. Add the strawberries and raspberries and continue to simmer for

10 minutes. Remove from the heat and cool for 15 minutes.

4 Remove the cinnamon stick. Ladle the mixture into 4-6 clear glasses. Wine glasses work well and look very pretty. Cover each glass with plastic wrap and refrigerate until well chilled. Serve the dessert chilled.

Prep time: 30 minutes plus chilling time
Good with: vanilla sauce (p 154)
Calories per serving: 311

Fruit Salad Gratinée
Dessert magic with leftovers

Feeds 4-5:

2½-3 pounds fruit (what's left in the fruit bowl, or anything that's appealing at the fruit stand—try for a mix of colors, but avoid citrus)

1/4 cup fresh lemon juice

2 eggs

2 tablespoons sugar

1/2 teaspoon grated lemon zest

1 teaspoon vanilla extract

1½ tablespoons almond or orange liqueur

1 Peel or wash the fruit, as appropriate, and chop it into small pieces. Drizzle the fruit with the lemon juice. Preheat the oven to 400°F.

2 Separate the egg yolks from the whites. In a bowl, whisk the yolks with the sugar, lemon zest, vanilla extract, and liqueur until smooth. In another bowl, whip the egg whites until stiff peaks form. Combine the whites with the yolk mixture and mix gently, but thoroughly.

3 Transfer the fruit salad to an ovenproof dish, spread the foamy egg mixture on top, and bake on the middle oven shelf for about 10 minutes, until lightly browned.

Prep time: 45 minutes
Good with: ladyfingers, sponge cake
Calories per serving: 390

Tip:
When beating egg whites, be sure that the bowl and whisk are very clean and oil free, or the egg whites will refuse to whip.

Orange Mousse
You'll want more

Feeds 6-8:

2 oranges

1 lemon

1½ envelopes unflavored gelatin

3 egg yolks

5 tablespoons sugar

1½ cups plain yogurt

3/4 cup heavy cream

Grated white chocolate and grated orange zest for garnish (optional)

1 Wash the oranges and lemon under hot water, then finely grate the zests. Cut the fruits in half and squeeze out the juice into a bowl. Sprinkle the gelatin over the juice and let stand for a few minutes.

2 Fill a wide saucepan halfway with water and heat to the simmering point, but do not boil. Now all you need is a tall metal mixing bowl that will fit into the pot without touching the water underneath. Put the yolks and sugar in the metal bowl and whisk until smooth, before placing it on the heat.

3 Now, set the metal bowl in the pot of hot water. Add the orange and lemon zest. Stir

the gelatin-juice mixture, add it to the bowl, and whisk continuously until the mixture is light and airy. Quickly remove the bowl from the heat.

4 Whisk the mixture , letting it cool briefly and mix in the yogurt. Chill for 5-10 minutes.

5 With a clean whisk, whip the cream until stiff peaks form, then gently fold the cream into the mousse base. Divide the mousse among 6 or 8 small molds or one large dish and chill well in the refrigerator until set. If you like, garnish with grated white chocolate and orange zest.

Prep time: 45 minutes, plus chilling time
Good with: sponge cake
Calories per serving (8): 440

Baked Apples
From Grandma's recipe box

Feeds 8:

2 tablespoons raisins

1/2 cup apple cider or juice

8 small, firm, tart apples, such as Granny Smith

2 tablespoons fresh lemon juice

2 tablespoons butter

2 ounces sliced almonds

1-2 tablespoons honey

1/4 teaspoon ground cinnamon

1-2 teaspoons grated lemon zest

1 Soak the raisins in the cider (or juice). Preheat the oven to 350°F.

2 Wash the apples well and wipe dry. Using an apple corer or paring knife, carefully cut out the apple cores—don't destroy the apple, but be sure to get the whole core. Drizzle the hollows with the lemon juice.

3 Smear an ovenproof dish with 1 teaspoon of the butter. Drain the raisins, pouring the cider (or juice) into the baking dish. Coarsely chop the almonds, and mix with the rest of the butter, the raisins, honey, cinnamon, and lemon zest.

4 Set the hollowed-out apples in the dish, and fill each one with the butter-almond mixture, dividing evenly. Bake the filled apples on the middle oven shelf for about 20 minutes, until tender.

Prep time: 45 minutes
Good with: vanilla ice cream or vanilla sauce (see page 154)
Calories per serving (8): 120

157

Fried Batter with Mascarpone
Different, but worth breaking your diet for

Feeds 3-4:

4 eggs

Pinch of salt

2½ tablespoons sugar

1 tablespoon grated lemon zest (from
3-4 lemons)

1/4 cup milk

1/2 cup flour

1 cup mascarpone cheese (look in a specialty
or Italian foods store)

2 tablespoons butter

Confectioners' sugar

1 Separate the yolks and whites of 2 of the eggs. Slide the 2 yolks into a mixing bowl. In another bowl, lightly beat the remaining 2 eggs and add them to the yolks. Add the salt, sugar, and lemon zest, and whisk. Whisk in first the milk, then the flour, then the mascarpone cheese.

2 In another clean bowl, whip the 2 egg whites until stiff peaks form. Fold the whipped egg whites gently and gradually into the yolk mixture—we're not looking for an evenly smooth mixture here, but a batter with clearly recognizable white streaks from the egg whites.

3 In a large skillet (don't use nonstick), melt the butter over medium heat. Pour the batter into the pan to make a layer an inch thick, and spread it smooth. Cook until the underside is set, when bubbles start forming on the surface. Then, take 2 knives, and scrape right through the batter, cutting it into small pieces.

4 Now heat the batter over high heat, using a spatula to toss until all the pieces are crispy and brown on the outside. Dust with confectioner's sugar and eat right away!

Prep time: 35 minutes
Good with: applesauce (you can buy it ready-made—or simply cook some peeled apple chunks just barely covered with water and lemon juice in a pan until soft; add sugar and cinnamon to taste), berry compote (see page 152), or another type of fruit compote.
Calories per serving (4): 555

Blueberry Muffins
An old trend is new again

Makes 12:

1¾ cups flour

1 tablespoon baking powder

1/4 teaspoon salt

1/2 pint (6 oz) fresh or frozen blueberries

1 egg

2/3 cup sugar

1 teaspoon vanilla extract

1/2 cup vegetable oil

2/3 cup buttermilk (milk, yogurt, or sour cream will work too)

1 Line a 12-cup muffin pan with paper muffin cups. If you don't have a muffin pan, put one paper liner inside another (times 12) and place on a baking sheet. Go ahead and preheat the oven to 350°F.

2 In a bowl, mix the flour, baking powder, and salt. Empty the blueberries into a colander and drain well (drink the juice or save it—you don't need it for this recipe).

3 In a mixing bowl, whisk the egg. Then, mix in the sugar, vanilla, oil, and buttermilk, and stir well. Gradually add the flour mixture, mixing just until moistened, then gently stir in the drained blueberries.

4 Divide the muffin batter among the muffin cups, filling about 3/4 full, and bake on the middle oven shelf for 20-25 minutes. Remove the muffins from the pan and eat them warm or cooled.

Prep time: busy 20 minutes, relaxing 20-25 minutes
Good with: vanilla sauce (see page 154), fruit butter
Calories per muffin: 210

Crêpes Suzette
Wafer-thin orange-flavored pancakes

Feeds 4:

2 tablespoons butter for the batter + 1

teaspoon for the orange sauce

2 eggs

2/3 cup milk

Pinch of salt

2 tablespoons sugar

1/2 cup flour

4 oranges

1 teaspoon vanilla extract

2 tablespoons orange liqueur (such as Grand Marnier or Cointreau)

1/4 cup confectioners' sugar

1 In a small pan, melt the 2 tablespoons butter, then remove from the heat. In a bowl, whisk the eggs with the milk, and add the salt and 1 tablespoon of the sugar. Add the flour in spoonfuls and stir to make a smooth, lump-free batter.

2 Squeeze the juice from 1/2 orange, and stir the juice into the melted butter in the pan. Pour the mixture into the batter, and stir until well blended. Cover and refrigerate for 30 minutes.

3 Wash one orange under hot water, dry, and grate the zest into a small bowl. Squeeze the juice from the zested orange and the orange half used for the batter into same bowl. Peel the thick layer of skin from 2 oranges until you hit fruit (be sure to remove all of the white "pith"). Then using a sharp knife, remove individual segments, cutting between the membranes and place in the bowl—be sure to save the juice that spills and add it to the rest.

4 Now for the orange sauce: In a medium skillet, melt the 1 teaspoon butter. Stir in the remaining 1 tablespoon sugar, and cook over medium heat until very light brown. Then, pour in the orange juice mixture, vanilla extract, and liqueur, and boil for 3-5 minutes, until syrupy. Keep warm over very low heat.

5 Brush a small nonstick skillet with melted butter and heat over medium heat. Stir the batter, then add a small ladleful to the pan, and swirl the pan so that the batter is evenly distributed. Cook for 1/2-1 minute, then turn, and cook for another 1/2-1 minute, until the crêpe is browned and cooked through. Fold up the crêpe into fourths, and lay it in the skillet with the orange sauce.

6 Cook the remaining batter in the same manner (remember to keep greasing the pan with butter and stir before ladling the batter each time). Fold up the remaining crêpes and lay them in the sauce. Dust the crêpes with confectioners' sugar and eat them right away with the sauce. You might want to heat them through in the sauce before eating.

Prep time: 1¼ hours
Good with: vanilla ice cream (for those with a real sweet tooth)
Calories per serving: 470

Tip:
For a richer sauce, stir in 1/4 cup butter off the heat.

Apple-Raisin Bread Pudding
This'll impress 'em

Feeds 6-8:

6 tablespoons butter

6 stale white dinner rolls or egg rolls

6 tablespoons sugar

4 medium-sized Granny Smith apples

1 lemon

2 cups milk

3 eggs

1 teaspoon vanilla extract

Pinch of salt

1/4 cup raisins

1/2 teaspoon ground cinnamon

2 tablespoons pine nuts

1 Preheat the oven to 400°F. Smear the bottoms and sides of large soufflé dish with 1 tablespoon of the butter.

2 Thinly slice the rolls. In a skillet, melt 3 tablespoons of the butter with 2 tablespoons of the sugar, stirring constantly. Spread the bread with the butter mixture, place on a baking sheet, and bake for 6 minutes. Peel, quarter, and core the apples. Cut the apples into wedges. Layer the bread and apples in the dish to resemble roof tiles.

3 Wash the lemon under hot water, dry it, and finely grate the zest. With a whisk, beat together the milk, zest, eggs, vanilla, salt, and the remaining 4 tablespoons sugar.

4 Pour the egg mixture over the apples and bread, and sprinkle with the raisins and cinnamon. Bake on the middle oven shelf for 30 minutes. Then, scatter the pine nuts and distribute pats of the remaining 2 tablespoons butter over the top. Bake for about 15 minutes, until the eggs are set.

Prep time: busy 30 minutes, relaxing 40-45 minutes
Good with: vanilla sauce (see p 154), vanilla ice cream
Calories per serving (8): 265

Lemon Tart
A basic from the Mediterranean

Feeds 8-10:

For the dough:

1¼ cups flour

3 tablespoons sugar

1/4 cup cold butter

Zest of 1/2 lemon

1 teaspoon vanilla extract

1 egg yolk

1 tablespoon ice water

For the filling:

1½ lemons

4 eggs

1 egg yolk

1/2 cup + 2 tablespoons sugar

1/2 cup heavy cream

1 tablespoon confectioners' sugar

Dried beans or peas and parchment paper for pre-baking the crust

1 To make the dough: toss the flour and sugar in a mixing bowl. Cut the butter into small pieces. Finely grate the lemon zest and add it to the flour mixture with the butter, vanilla, egg yolk, and water.

2 Wash your hands in cold water to keep the dough from heating too much while working with it. Place the dough mixture on a work surface and gently knead it until no more pieces of butter can be seen. Form the dough into a ball and place it between 2 large pieces of plastic wrap. With a rolling pin, roll out the dough into a 10- or 11-inch circle. Partially wrap the dough around the rolling pin and carefully transfer it to a 9- or 10-inch pie dish. Press the dough into the pan and cut off the edges with a knife. Refrigerate for 1 hour.

3 Preheat the oven to 350°F. Place a piece of foil on top of the dough and fill it with pie weights, or dried peas or beans. Prebake the dough on the middle oven shelf for about 10 minutes. Cool.

4 To make the filling: wash the lemons under hot water, dry, and grate the zest. Squeeze the juice from the lemons. Place the eggs and egg yolk in a bowl and whisk until really foamy. Add the lemon zest and juice and whisk well. In another bowl, whip the cream until stiff peaks form and fold them into the filling mixture.

5 Reduce the oven heat to 300°F. Remove the weights, beans, or peas from the cooled, prebaked dough. Pour the lemon filling onto the dough and spread evenly. Bake for 50 minutes, until the filling is set.

6 Cool the tart completely. Before serving, turn on the broiler. Dust the tart with confectioners' sugar and broil until brown. Careful—it could take less than a minute!

Prep time: busy 35 minutes, relaxing 1½ hours
Good with: espresso
Calories per serving (10): 340

Chocolate Mousse
The "Old Faithful" of desserts

Feeds 4-6:

9 ounces semisweet chocolate

1/4 cup butter

5 super-fresh eggs

Salt

2 tablespoons sugar

1 Here's yet another recipe that uses a water bath—so half-fill a fairly large saucepan with water and heat until simmering. Find a metal bowl that sits inside of the pan so that the bottom doesn't touch the water.

2 Finely chop the chocolate and put it in a small saucepan with the butter. Heat over low heat until the mixture is melted and smooth. Remove from the heat.

3 Separate the whites and yolks of the eggs. In a clean bowl, whip the egg whites with a pinch of salt until stiff peaks form. Put the egg yolks and sugar in the metal bowl. Set the bowl in a pot of ice-cold water (for a change) and beat until foamy. Then, move the bowl to the warm water bath and beat until the mixture is thick and creamy.

4 The Grande Finale: Stir the chocolate mixture into the foamy eggs . Then, add just 1/3 of the egg whites and mix well. Now, gently fold in the rest of the egg whites, but don't really mix them in too much—leave it nice and airy. Fill little dishes or wine glasses with the mousse and chill well (at least 3 hours in refrigerator).

Prep time: 30-40 minutes (depends on practice and experience with water bath), plus chilling time
Good with: whipped cream, fresh berries
Calories per serving: 535

The Basics-Glossary-That Isn't

I'll bet you've noticed that we haven't written stuff like "deglaze" or "bain marie" in our cooking instructions. That's because we wanted everyone to understand what we mean.

Most of the cookbook is written in a straightforward way for once, without all the usual bla bla bla that's in other cookbooks. It's like drinking sparkling water after a long night of oversized martinis and double espressos. It's just a cookbook. But, you ask, "What's with the title, 'Basic cooking?'" Chill—does everything always have to be spelled out? Seems you've understood everything so far—or you would never have made it to the last page. You've arrived at our multi-purpose glossary: it covers things that don't appear in Basic Cooking, helpful tips for reading and understanding other cookbooks, and the stuff that happens when the cooking's done and we're eating and drinking and that has to do with the accompanying small talk (see heading.)

Alcohol
Can make—or break—a whole party. To avoid the latter, try to cut any corners on quality, not quantity.

Apéritif
A mild appetite-stimulating alcoholic drink. Sparkling wine or champagne is a good choice, but you can also pour the same white wine that's going to be served at table, provided it's on the light side. Other typical aperitifs: Campari, Lillet, Dubonnet. Strong brandies are not good. Classic slip of the tongue: "Now that we've eaten, let's have a nice apéritif."

Baking
Quite a different ball game and rarely a passionate cook's strong point. That's why it hardly comes up in this book (but it's in the works).

Blanching
Plunging something in boiling water to precook it. Sometimes you then "shock" the item in ice cold water to lock in its bright color.

Carving
Refers to slicing roasted meats or poultry into serving pieces. If done right, it can be impressive when performed at the dinner table. If you blow it (i.e. flinging a chicken leg onto the lap of your best friend's dinner date), the entire evening is at serious risk.

Deglazing
After browning something, add liquid and scrape off any browned bits stuck to the bottom of the pan or pot for the sauce. Smart: just when the guests peer into the kitchen, add a generous shot of good red wine to the pan for dramatic sizzling effect. Stupid: dropping the bottle because you got overexcited.

Diet
We use the Seven-Day Basics Diet: eat what you like for a week—but never the same thing twice.

Glazing
Sautéing vegetables with oil or butter, liquid, and some sugar so until they're cooked through and coated with a glossy syrup.

Glasses
It's really true: the glass you drink from affects the taste of the drink (if you doubt it, try drinking coffee from first a thick then a thin cup). Also true: the finer the drink, the finer the differences. It's best to sip champagne from a long tall flute, rather than slurp it from a squatty wide glass. Also important: the glass sits to the right of the plate; don't forget water glass; never fill wine glasses more than half full.

Gossip
"My God, what an awful evening. As soon as one person got up to leave, the others scuttled after him." "So why did you end up being the last to leave?" "So the same thing doesn't happen to me one day." A bit of gossip spices up dinner. But too much spoils the appetite. See also Small Talk.

Gratinée, Au Gratin
Refers to a baked dish with a browned crust on top.

Hands and Fingers
Ideal tools for kneading, mixing salads (not at the table please), tasting to test the seasoning (again, only if no one's looking), and welcoming guests (wash them first). Eating with your hands is easier in some cases (think sandwiches, chicken legs) and in other cases more sensual (think asparagus, shellfish, strawberries) than eating with utensils. Smart idea: always keep one hand clean.

Manners
It never hurts to get things right. Always good: please, thank you, apologies (though not overdone). Not so good: being excessively pretentious at spontaneous occasions (it just makes other people uncomfortable). Never good: talking too loudly and showering people when you talk, sneezing, belching and worse.

Marinate

To immerse something in a seasoned liquid in order to infuse it with flavor and tenderize.

Menu Planning

Include a salad before the main dish and/or a dessert after, and you've got a planned menu. Rule Number One: Don't overdo it. If friends just want a quick snack before a movie, don't plan a six-course menu. And don't stand in the kitchen cussing for half an hour between courses—that's a real conversation-stopper. Rule Number Two: Variety is the spice of good cooking, too. Cream soup, chicken cutlets in cream sauce, and a whipped cream-based dessert doesn't have enough variety to be interesting.

Mom's Cooking

Can animate or be the kiss of death to dinner conversation Here's an example: "The last time I tasted a roast this good was at my mother's." This animates conversation if the cook doesn't have any hang-ups about his or her age; it can cause the other guests to also start reminiscing. It's the kiss of death if your partner, who regularly cooks the roast at your house, is at the table.

Napkins

Are useful even for a midnight snack, as long as they are not damask origami swans, doomed to kill off any spontaneity and get your guests wondering how long you've been fumbling around with their napkins.

Perfume

The tongue is only capable of recognizing the basic taste of a dish; the nose is the one that picks up the nuances. If everyone around the table agrees that tonight everything somehow tastes of musk and/or violets, someone probably overdid it at the vanity. Even worse: perfumed candles and lamp oils. See also Smoking.

Poaching

Lightly cooking something in nearly boiling water. See also Simmering.

Silverware

Usually helpful. A knife (right of the plate) and fork (left of the plate) are your basic eating utensils; a spoon, if required, sits to right of the knife. If it's a big affair with several courses, eat from the outside in. It's always a thrill to see a little spoon perched above the plate (handle to the right), hinting at something sweet to come. On the rise: chopsticks (sit parallel on right of the dish, or diagonal in front of the plate.) See Hands.

Simmering

A liquid is simmering when it's just below boiling point and little bubbles rise to the surface.

Slurping

Wine connoisseurs and espresso drinkers know that slurping improves an already good glass of wine or cup of coffee, since it accentuates the bouquet. And within the privacy of your own four walls, the sound of satisfied slurping from the soup dish can be an ode to the culinary art. Nevertheless: if in doubt, an honest compliment tends to get the message across more clearly.

Small Talk

It's OK to get a successful evening underway, but it can be rather staid for dinner conversation. Good topics: the weather, TV, sports, entertainment, food, drinks. Bad topics: natural disasters, the Bible, diseases, politics, digestion problems, drinking stories. See also Mother's Cooking.

Smoking

Though it can be a delicate subject, there's no doubt about it: smoking and tasting just don't get along. Which is why you should only smoke if lighting up a cigarette—or whatever—is important to everyone. Otherwise: if it's okay, smoke before or after eating. Or excuse yourself and go outside for your smoke—remember to pick up the butts after you are through. Or, if it's a big affair, look for designated smoking places in between courses.

Stock

Hearty liquid usually made from meat bones, fish bones, and/or vegetables. It's an excellent base for sauces and soups. You can make it or buy it. Also called broth.

Stuffing

Very finely chopped mixture of meat, fish, or vegetables used as filling.

Sweating (onions or garlic)

Lightly sautéing until translucent, without letting the items brown.

Zest

The colored part of citrus fruit peels. Scrape off the white stuff on the underside to avoid bitter flavors.

Basic Index A - Z

164

Credits

The Authors:

Jennifer Newens

...is an ex-restaurant professional and current cookbook editor, serious food lover, messy cook, and she moved from New York to San Francisco while working on this book

...likes lemon best juiced for salad dressings and marinades, and zested to add intriguing flavor to both savory and sweet dishes

...loves lots of mini-meals for dinner, and someone to wash the dishes after she cooks

...was involved in many aspects of creating Basic Cooking, e.g., developing recipes, writing text, editing, and food styling

Sebastian Dickhaut

...is a journalist, cook, adoptive Austrian, seriously curious, a tad old-fashioned, and he relocated from Munich to Sydney while working on this book

...likes lemon best with chicken of all shapes and sizes, in his Mom's stock, in iced-tea with ginger and mint, and in anything and everything sweet

...loves lunch served till midnight and rustling up surprise dishes from ingredients in the refrigerator and pantry

...helped turn the Basic Cooking idea into reality and wrote the captions for the book

Sabine Sälzer

... wound up authoring a cookbook thanks to chance and passion, isn't always infinitely patient but is relentlessly optimistic, and also moved while working on this book

...likes lemon to rescue dishes that taste dull

...loves full cupboards and always buys too much at the store

...can't say no to Viennese sausages—it's the mustard. Can say no to something thrown together without caring

...helped conceive the Basic Cooking idea and wrote many of the recipes

Photography

Germany:
Food photographs: Barbara Bonisolli
People photographs: Alexander Walter
Recipe stylist: Hans Gerlach
Models: Gabie Ismaier, Markus Röleke, Janna Sälzer, Kai Schröter

U.S.:
Photographs: Lisa Keenan
Models: David Mabry, Sandra Luiz Nascimento, Jennifer Newens, Jennifer Wofford
Props courtesy of Sur la Table

Photo Credits
Barbara Bonisolli: recipe photos, step photos, cooking methods, the "17 staples" and the "14 essentials"

Alexander Walter: people pictures, except where noted below; still-life feature photo, page 7 and page 134

Lisa Keenan: crab cakes, page 113, eggplant, page 145, marinated shrimp, page 77, spicy broccoli, page 146, tuna tartare, page 107, fish photo, page 102. People pictures, pages 2, 3, 8, 9, 11, 40, 42, 52, 68, 69, 70, 82, 119, 120, 121, 124, 134, 140, 145, 167, back cover

Stock Photos
Walter Pfister: noodles pages 38 and 40 / Picture Box: onion pages 66 and 116 / Maximilian Stock: tomato page 132 and page 135; egg page 10, page 84 and page 86; fish page 100; apple page 151 / Gerhard Bumann: carrot page 135.
S. & P. Eising: cream page 148
Michael Boyney: page 168 above

German Team:

Editor: Katharina Lisson
Reader: Cornelia Schinharl
Layout and design: Sybille Engels and Thomas Jancovic
Production: Susanne Mühldorfer
Set: Filmset Schröter
Repro: Fotolito Longo
Printing and binding: Druckhaus Kaufmann

Thank you to Christa Schmedes, Erdmute Albat and Klaus Neumann, Ulla Thomsen, Siemens, Monopol, Rösle, WMF and Zassenhaus

U.S. Team:

Editor: Jennifer Newens, CCP
Art Director: Shanti Nelson
Translator: Jacolyn Harmer
Recipe Developer: Jennifer Newens, CCP
Recipe Tester: Janis B. Judd, CCP
Reader: Vené Franco

Thank you to Larry Keenan, Lois and Curt Nelson, Patti Rader, Heather Sparks Casting

Published originally under the title
BASIC COOKING:
Alles, was man braucht, um schnell gut zu kochen

© 1999 Gräfe und Unzer Verlag Gmbh, München

English translation copyright:
© 2000, Silverback Books, Inc.

ISBN: 1-930603-00-2

Printed in Hong Kong